Leading Groups to Solutions

A practical guide for facilitators
and team members.

Steven J. Stowell, Ph.D.
Joel F. McCausland
Stephanie S. Mead

CMOE Press
Salt Lake City, UT

CMOE, Inc.
9146 South 700 East
Sandy, UT 84070

ISBN # 0-9724627-0-8

First Edition
First Printing, November 2002

Editing: Helen Hodgson & Emily Burr
Copyediting and Word Processing: Debbie Stowell and Linda Latimer
Cover Design: Amanda Wilson and Margaret Landvatter
Graphic Design: Design Type Service

This book and other CMOE publications are available by ordering direct from the publisher.

CMOE Press
(801) 569-3444
www.cmoe.com

ACKNOWLEDGEMENTS

A book about leading groups to solutions would be impossible to write without a fertile environment in which to test our ideas. With this in mind, we wish to thank:

✦ Our valued clients and partners, who have been willing to experiment and explore our theories and methodologies.

✦ The fantastic team at The Center for Management and Organization Effectiveness (CMOE), where every day we are faced with the opportunity and the challenge to make these principles live in our own interactions.

✦ Emily Burr for her editing work and ability to create a stimulating reading experience.

✦ Linda Latimer, for tireless work and preparation of the many drafts of this book.

✦ Deb Hedgepeth for her efforts to get this book launched.

✦ Helen Hodgson, whose expertise and insights as editor brought structure and coherence to our ideas.

✦ Our families, who provide continued support, patience, and encouragement for all of our endeavors.

TABLE OF CONTENTS

CHAPTER 1

Sooner
or Later

CHAPTER 1

Sooner or Later

Sooner or later, everyone works in a group, perhaps as a team member, but perhaps leading, coordinating, or facilitating one. It doesn't matter if the facilitator is a designated manager, coach, spiritual leader, Girl Scout leader, or a leader selected more informally.

This book is for anyone who is a member of a group and wants to get things accomplished. This book is not about managing meetings, nor is it about how to present or speak in front of a group. It's not about how to train or teach people, although this can be part of the process. This book is about how to get people to sit down and collaborate, problem solve, plan, organize, and make decisions. It addresses the collaborative process of building consensus, creating synergy, and harnessing collective energy to create innovative solutions. It is about combining the best individual thinking into one, focused effort, about creating shared commitment, so that the implementation of solutions is supported and sustained long term.

"The future is a collective effort. You can't decide on the future alone, and you especially can't create it alone."

Faith Popcorn

Whether organizing a food drive for the needy or trying to establish scientific standards to measure global warming, people may become members of a high-performance, intact work team or serve on a deeply divided, politically charged school board. Regardless of the goals or challenges faced by the group, learning to navigate through the twists, turns, ups, and downs can be the driving force that helps the group get things done. People can exert a powerful and positive influence when they understand how the game is played and have a feel for the terrain.

The sad fact is that most people don't. Everyone attends meetings — far too many in most cases. People serve on committees, attend staff meetings, and hold meetings to plan other meetings. Sometimes life seems to be spent in meetings. The frequent criticisms of meetings — they're boring, not focused, and a waste of time — are all too often accurate. But with the right road map, skills, and perspective, that can change. People can learn what it takes to successfully lead, coordinate, and facilitate lasting change and genuine progress as the best contributions of each team member are utilized.

Each group has its own unique personality. Individual viewpoints, experiences, and perspectives blend together to create a diverse mix of people. Some team members come to meetings and discussions with hidden, and not-so-hidden, agendas. Some may be unable or unwilling to view situations from any viewpoint but their own myopic perspective. Team members naturally coalesce, drifting into sub-groups and cliques that can be divisive and distracting. Groups frequently fall into a pattern of "group think," or collusion, that limits free expression and critical self-examination.

> "When you first assemble a group, it's not a team right off the bat. It's only a collection of individuals."
>
> *Mike Krzyzewski*

How many times, as a team member, has it felt uncomfortable or even unsafe to truly speak your mind? How many times have you felt the need to edit your thoughts and say what you think someone else wants to hear? How often have you seen others protect themselves by saying only what is politically correct? When trust is low, essential issues don't surface. And when the real issues aren't addressed, sooner or later, every team member pays the price for bad group work. It may be as simple as not capturing and leveraging all the information, experience, or talent team members have to offer. It may be that the best ideas aren't always implemented, because they have not been heard. Or problems may arise later, when doubts, lack of commitment, and failure to reach consensus make it impossible for the group to follow through on plans and achieve its goals. It isn't easy helping a group say what needs to be said. In every organization and culture, taboos, past history, and even obvious weaknesses can be difficult to discuss. But effective groups encourage honest dialogue, build a broad, deep pool of information, and courageously and constructively confront hard issues.

Effective groups concentrate on *what* is right, not on *who* is right. Members in these groups learn when to listen and when to contribute. Meetings aren't a competition to see who can be the most clever or insightful. Rather, meetings represent a commitment to achieve the best results.

This book addresses the issues and challenges that groups commonly face as they seek to find creative solutions, launch new initiatives, and create high-performing teams. The book also explores models and tools to enable skilled facilitators to help groups achieve their goals.

Tips for Team Members

Everyone will have an opportunity to lead or facilitate the work of a group at some point. It might be an official assignment at work or involvement in a civic, family, or church activity. Whether you act as an official leader or as a participant, knowing how to help groups get things done is a valuable skill, applicable to several aspects of your life.

Prepare to Lead

✔ Evaluate your own readiness to lead. Can you communicate well with groups? Do you convey your message in a compelling way?

Get Involved and Contribute

✔ What teams or groups do you belong to?

✔ What can you do to get more involved?

Support the Decisions of Your Team

✔ Do you feel aligned with the teams or groups you belong to?

✔ Do you walk away from team meetings energized and ready to contribute, or feeling disconnected and unexcited by their plans?

CHAPTER 2

How This Book Works

CHAPTER 2

How This
Book Works

I n preparing to write this book, we tested our ideas about facilitating
the work of teams. We discussed, debated, and argued the merits
of various approaches and theories. In the development of this book,
 we reviewed what we've learned over the past 55 combined years of work with clients, and we put our own facilitation skills and processes to the test. Even the writing and editing of the book required that we "walk our
own talk" in resolving differences, defining priorities, and
creating a coherent message.

We've made a commitment at The Center for Management and
Organization Effectiveness (CMOE) to model our material, to be a
representative of what we teach to others, and to act the same way we
teach our clients to act. And while we're not perfect, we are pleased
with the culture of acceptance, accountability, synergy, cooperation,
and challenge that exists at CMOE.

Over the years, through research and client work, we've observed
a lot of behavior and feel that we've learned a few things about what
makes an effective team. We believe that the principles and suggestions in this book help everyone who spends time in teams. Whether
leading, participating as a team member, or both, you will find that
this book provides a framework for building effective teams.

Part I of this book introduces a model that serves as a roadmap
when facilitating, or leading groups to solutions. Facilitating isn't an
exact process; rather, it is fluid and dynamic. Group situations that

require facilitation come in cycles and require flexibility and fluctuation in style and approach. The interactive waves vary in size, intensity, and shape. Some are small and difficult to recognize; others are so large that they threaten to swamp the ship. This model helps facilitators navigate through all types of group situations.

Part II of the book examines specific skills that apply to each wave. Some "how-to's" are provided to enhance facilitation abilities or the ability of team members to contribute.

It's important to recognize that leaders are also team members. For this reason, we've devoted some thought, and space in this book, to a special section entitled "Tips for Team Members." This simple summary, found at the end of most chapters, provides the facilitator and team members with helpful, practical tips on how to better contribute, even when you're not in charge. Team members learn how to support the efforts of the facilitator, lead the group to solutions when circumstances dictate, and help other team members make a contribution.

> It's important to recognize that leaders are also team members.

As writers, we really enjoyed collaborating on this project because it gave us another opportunity to use these skills as we facilitated through our own group discussions. The intention of the model and ideas in this book is to open eyes and minds to new perspectives and approaches. We are confident that you will find these skills valuable in every group endeavor.

Tips for Team Members

This book isn't meant to explore and exhaust every topic related to working with groups. What it's meant to do is to provide some practical tips and steps team members and leaders can take to combine their best efforts, use synergy in developing innovative solutions, and communicate clearly and effectively.

Read This Book!

✔ This book provides a comprehensive look at how to work more effectively within groups. You will learn about facilitation and leadership skills, and how to participate as a team member.

✔ The "Tips for Team Members" feature appears at the end of most chapters, providing specific questions and ideas for group members interested in making a greater contribution.

Put Yourself in the Facilitator's Shoes

✔ Do you understand the challenges your team or group provides to its leaders?

✔ Have you ever been in charge of getting a group to accomplish something?

✔ What can you do to support the efforts of your group's leader?

CHAPTER 3

Sometimes the Best Ideas . . . Aren't

Sometimes the Best Ideas . . . Aren't

A recent newspaper article provides a real-world example of the challenges inherent in group problem-solving. The U.S. military recently launched a project to develop a high-tech infantry system known as the "Land Warrior." The goal of the system was to provide an individual soldier with the latest and greatest in weaponry, communications, and protection. The Land Warrior was supposed to include innovations such as the following:

✦ Global Positioning System (GPS) to eliminate the need for paper maps and other navigational tools

✦ Heat-sensing thermal sights, enabling soldiers to spot the enemy at distances up to 300 meters

✦ Helmets with "heads-up" video display and a built-in radio with antenna, microphone, and speaker

✦ Heavy-duty, bulletproof body armor

✦ Eye protection against ballistic laser weapons

✦ Personal computer complete with mouse, touch-screen, and keyboard providing access to wireless e-mail, secure reports, and possibly cable TV

✦ Protective knee and elbow pads

✦ Rifle with daytime video and nighttime thermal sights and combat optics

✦ Video camera allowing soldiers to peer around corners or out of foxholes without exposing themselves to enemy fire

The system also incorporated the basics of a foot soldier's life, such as ammunition, food, water, clothing, boots, etc.

The Land Warrior was touted as the kind of revolutionary, cutting-edge thinking that universities, research centers, factories, and businesses around the world could use to leap into the new millennium. The only problem with the Land Warrior was that it didn't work.

Oh, the technology was sound, and the individual devices within the system operated effectively. But the finished prototype weighed over 40 pounds (18 kilograms). The Land Warrior was intended to help troops on the ground fight more effectively and safely. In the conceptual stage, military leaders wanted to utilize the latest and most powerful technology. However, designers and testers of the system soon found that including all the gadgets resulted in a cumbersome, awkward system that was functionally useless in the field — not to mention its development cost of over $2 billion, over twice initial estimates. The Land Warrior essentially became a fiscal and political nightmare.

In theory, the Land Warrior is an awesome fighting machine. Imagine the power of a fully integrated, electronically linked team on the battlefield. It sounds like a great idea. But in practice, the system exhibited a host of problems, some inconvenient and some potentially fatal.

During initial testing, soldiers who rolled on the ground (a common maneuver) got stuck on their backs like tortoises. The helmet was so heavy that troops couldn't lift their heads to fire the high-tech rifle. The radio and video cables snagged in trees and brush. Soldiers eventually ripped the system off in exhaustion and frustration, effectively cutting off their communication link.

> "No matter how high or excellent technology may be . . . unless the group of human beings which compromise the enterprise work together toward one unified goal, the enterprise is sure to go down the path of decline."
>
> *Takashi Ishihara*

Other problems surfaced as well. The computer and radio batteries drained rapidly, and the software proved unreliable. Add to this the prospect of bailing out of an airplane with this bulky monstrosity or crossing a deep stream loaded down with all the sensitive electronic gear. Ironically, there didn't seem to be room for a parachute or SCUBA equipment.

How did the Land Warrior system become such a mess? How did this exciting and potentially powerful concept become such a failure in practice? Where did the creative, problem-solving process go wrong?

There are likely more reasons than can be identified, but it seems clear that something went wrong between theory and practice. Albert Einstein once said, "A problem cannot be solved with the mind that created it." The development of the Land Warrior is a classic example of trying to create new solutions with old paradigms. A lack of creativity, critical thinking, reflection, and introspection, as well as not enough testing to find out if the systems would really work, contributed to the Land Warrior debacle.

This example isn't meant as an indictment of the U.S. military. The fact is, these problems happen every day, in groups and organizations of all sizes. And the costs are staggering.

Groups fail in their objectives for a variety of reasons. Instead of lacking in creativity, groups simply don't draw the *best* ideas out of the members. They fail not for lack of commitment, but for lack of a process for decision-making and problem-solving that harnesses the talents of individual team members. Most groups have the best of intentions, but they don't know how to translate intent into productive practice.

Leaders of teams have a special responsibility to regulate, focus, and guide the efforts of team members. High-performing groups have been the birthplace of major breakthroughs and innovations. When people work closely together, collaborate, and find synergy, great things are possible.

But synergy doesn't happen automatically, or just by gathering people together. Synergy has to be actively developed. The average group contains too much ego, competitiveness, and personal and professional pride, as well as varying interests and agendas, to become a focused and effective force. Someone at some time has to step back, observe the patterns and dynamics, ask the tough questions, and exert influence on the way individual team members are working together.

In the case of the Land Warrior, a whole new group was required to study the problem and create a new solution. Facing pressure from Congress to kill the program, the new team had to act quickly to find a new approach to the project. The new team reassessed the original specifications, tossed out some of the assumptions and concepts that had guided the original group, reconsidered traditional suppliers, threw out four-years of work, and overhauled their thinking. They developed new concepts and new ways of working to create an affordable, functional, and reliable system.

The new partnership learned to manage conflict, set their egos aside, and get the technical thinkers to synergize. They slapped together a crude model, avoiding a lengthy and expensive prototype phase. Rather than building everything from scratch or trying to reinvent the wheel, the new group chose proven and familiar components, and integrated them into a functional system.

Remarkably, in only six months, the new team delivered a streamlined prototype at half the price of the bulky original. The new unit weighed only 12 pounds, and the onboard computer ran for 10 days on one battery charge. It only took the Army one day to make its decision. The new team won a $35 million contract to deliver more prototypes, an agreement that may lead to a long-term, $18 billion deal with the military to manufacture and repair the Land Warrior.

If the U.S. Army and its suppliers can change their ways, then facilitators and organizations can learn to manage change, create new solutions, and

> If the U.S. Army and its suppliers can change their ways, then facilitators and organizations can learn to manage change, create new solutions, and harness talents and ideas in innovative ways.

harness talents and ideas in innovative ways. The challenge of change is formidable. Every organization has its own way of interacting and its own patterns, habits, and policies. Most groups must deal with negative attitudes, political infighting, turf battles, and uncompromising egomaniacs.

Organizations need people with the skills, processes, and tools necessary to navigate through the storms and choppy water. The chaos  of constant change requires bright and dedicated people to contribute all of their knowledge, skills, courage, and experience when addressing important issues.

It can be done. Groups can become effective "land warriors" against all the natural enemies that the organization faces. As leaders, or team members, individuals can help teams become a powerful force for change, rather than the butt of jokes, the object of cynicism, or an example of inefficiency.

Developing the skills to lead groups to positive change requires patience. Facilitators have to be willing to look beneath the surface to see what's really happening within the group. In the chapters to come, facilitators and team members will learn how to effectively observe group interactions, patterns, and styles. They will also learn how to evaluate the group's strengths and weaknesses and find ways to neutralize the negative while building on positive characteristics and dynamics.

Even team members (anyone who is not the formal leader of a group) can exert a great deal of influence. The processes and tools in this book prove valuable in every kind of group interaction. Leadership is a shared responsibility. Regardless of title or assignment, everyone can contribute to the growth and development of groups. And when the time comes to formally lead a group, team members are prepared.

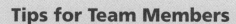

Tips for Team Members

This chapter explores a vivid example of what can happen when teams or groups work without clear vision, don't have parameters for success, and get caught in "group think." When teams fail to engage the best, most creative, and independent thought its members are capable of, the results can be disappointing.

Speak Up: Avoid Group Think

✔ Does your team or group enjoy open discussion about the issues that affect you?

✔ Can you say what you really think without fear?

✔ Are you personally willing to voice opposite or even unpopular opinions?

Exercise Your Creativity

✔ Are you giving your best thinking and efforts to your team?

✔ Do you feel engaged and excited by the work you do with your groups?

✔ What opportunities to be more involved can you identify? Which of your talents can you use to help your team?

Facilitating Solutions: Models and Tools

Facilitating Solutions: Models and Tools

There are as many ways to facilitate groups as there are problems, projects, and challenges that need to be facilitated. Some approaches fail to deliver desired results within the required budgetary, time, and organizational constraints. Some highly task-focused approaches deliver results, but at the expense of relationships within the group. Ideally, a skilled facilitator crafts an approach that helps the group achieve its goals while building and maintaining trust, synergy, and team chemistry.

Leading groups to solutions requires a deep understanding of the issues and an ability to draw out the best thinking, most effort, and strongest commitment possible from the group. Successful facilitators understand the make-up of the group and the individual talents, personalities, strengths, weaknesses, and blind spots of the team members. Effective facilitators learn to dampen personal agendas and preferences, allowing the group to discover and create solutions that team members feel ownership for and are willing to pursue in the face of the inevitable pressures and challenges that arise.

What is a Facilitator?

The word "facilitator" conjures images of an outside consultant or trainer who conducts training or brainstorming sessions. In fact, many training professionals prefer the term "facilitator" over "instructor" because they believe their role is not just to share information, but to help groups discover new ideas for themselves and relate these lessons to real-life challenges.

The role of a facilitator, while not always expressly stated in the job description, falls more often to the team leader or manager than to any other person. Many managers aren't prepared for or accustomed to acting in the facilitator role. They may not have the foggiest idea of how to effectively *lead* teams to solutions. When faced with a problem or challenge, their tendency is to make an immediate decision or to solve the problem first and then announce the solution to the team. It may not even occur to some people to involve the team in working through and discovering solutions. After all, isn't the job of the manager to take charge, lead the way, and come up with brilliant answers to every question?

It can require a significant shift in perspective for a team leader or manager, particularly one accustomed to more of a "command and control" management style, to take on a guiding role, rather than a directive one. Some leaders take to it naturally; others need time to re-frame their role, assumptions, and beliefs, and to test out a facilitative approach. Regardless of the starting point, the facilitative leader ultimately realizes some practical and pleasant benefits:

> "Men pay no attention to a dog that is always barking."
>
> Margaret L. Clement

✦ Reduced stress, because he/she doesn't have to personally resolve every problem

✦ Increased team-member capabilities as they take responsibility for solutions

✦ Increased sense of team unity and shared purpose

✦ A more inclusive and open team

Members of teams led by true facilitators have the following experiences:

✦ Begin to see their position less as a job and more as an opportunity to contribute and influence the organization

✦ Feel more valued as the facilitator draws out their ideas, and yes, even as they are asked to take on increased responsibility

✦ Gain practical experience and develop new skills

✦ Provide innovative and creative ideas, perspectives, and solutions

✦ Feel more challenged to think creatively

✦ Cooperate with team members

✦ Constructively resolve differences and disagreements

What is Facilitation?

Facilitation is a substantially neutral process of effectively coordinating the problem-solving activities of a group, and helping to achieve a common purpose while maintaining a balance between the tasks and relationships.

A facilitator reflects the "will" of the group, doesn't over-control choices or procedures, and maximizes the involvement of team members. A facilitator helps the group raise uncomfortable or often avoided issues and topics, and addresses them in an open, constructive, and supportive fashion. A facilitator keeps a group moving forward while building consensus and achieving synergy among team members.

Elements of Facilitation

Facilitators can employ a process to effectively approach facilitation opportunities with a group or team. These skills, or "waves" of facilitation, help establish structure for sometimes complex projects and tasks. However, there are other underlying elements to consider and prepare for as well — keys that provide a universal foundation for effective facilitation. These generally fall into one of three categories: task, behavior, and climate.

Task

Task refers to the work to be done. Whether the issue is the launch of a new product line or a policy that needs to be re-visited, "task" refers to an item that the group takes responsibility to see through to completion. A facilitated experience that doesn't produce results, in definable and assignable tasks, is just a discussion.

Task is the centerpiece of facilitation. The task or action plan that results from an effective facilitation process is clearly defined and specifically assigned to and accepted by team members. Each task is clearly linked and integrated with other tasks, and has a specific timetable for completion. When there is clarity around tasks and responsibilities, the project has a much greater chance of success.

Task also has to do with the standards, guidelines, and organizational goals that relate to the group or project at hand. The task must align with the overriding issues and priorities of the division, department, or organization. Addressing the task is not something that is accomplished once in a meeting or discussion; it usually requires focus and attention over time. Task begins when groups realize that they have something to accomplish, and the task is the central focus of the discussion to clarify the problem and create a plan for a resolution. Progress and evaluation are measured against how well the demands of the task have been met.

Behavior

Behavior refers to the specific actions of the facilitator. No factor is perhaps as critical to success of the group as the way the facilitator communicates, listens, and sets the tone for the group's interactions. In each wave of facilitation, specific, purposeful facilitator behaviors ensure inclusion of team members. Appropriate facilitator behavior draws out the best thinking, provides an accurate evaluation, creates a workable solution, and effectively manages group dynamics.

Behavior represents personal actions, language, and attitudes.

> No factor is perhaps as critical to success of the group as the way the facilitator communicates, listens, and sets the tone for the group's interactions.

Sometimes, behavior refers to things that a facilitator doesn't do, as well as the things he or she does. Behavior is the role the facilitator assumes, the approach that's chosen, the tone that is set.

Examples of positive facilitator behavior include the following:

✦ Showing enthusiasm for ideas

✦ Being an active listener

✦ Withholding judgment and maintaining neutrality as the discussion unfolds

✦ Observing, recognizing, and managing early warning signs of disruption, tension, and conflict

✦ Maintaining energy within the group

✦ Being open-minded, accepting, and flexible

✦ Asking useful, thought-provoking, and probing questions

✦ Helping the group discuss issues that need to be explored

✦ Monitoring the climate of the group

The behavior the facilitator chooses to employ has more to do with the ultimate success or failure of the endeavor than any other factor. A skilled facilitator can encourage, inspire, and help a group work through to solutions they might never have arrived at by themselves. A skilled facilitator can rescue a discussion teetering on the brink of disaster or getting mired in hostility, distrust, and skepticism. A skilled facilitator finds ways to build relationships, while delivering the results demanded by stakeholders.

Climate

Climate is the environment in which the facilitation occurs. This is the third overarching concept of facilitation, and its success depends on the willingness and cooperation of team members. Climate is usually a result of several different factors:

✦ The overall culture and climate of the organization

✦ The level of trust enjoyed (or not enjoyed) by team members

✦ Time and other demands to get the problem solved or project completed

✦ The prevailing management style

✦ The team's record of past successes or failures

It is important to recognize that climate is a combination of several factors. Some of the factors that weigh in, such as the current financial health of the organization or legal issues, might be outside the group's control. Other factors, however, like the respect that team members demonstrate to one another, are completely controlled by the group.

Climate is a way of life for a particular group. It is the patterns, habits, and agreements that have grown up among them, and which represent their values, beliefs, and priorities. In a positive climate, team members feel and express a genuine desire to work effectively together, a willingness to address difficult topics without personal offense, and a unity of spirit and purpose. Negative climates, on the other hand, are characterized by adverse feelings, resentment, and grudges by team members who resist cooperation (and may in fact work against one another), and by the formation of destructive cliques and sub-groups with other agendas.

A positive climate has certain characteristics:

✦ Members are involved and interested in the task.

✦ Collaboration is high; individual competitiveness is low.

✦ Everyone's contribution is recognized and valued.

✦ Conflicts are resolved openly and honestly.

✦ Differences are welcomed, and not taken personally.

✦ Members are relaxed, not stressed, or under extreme tension. There may be tension regarding the task or topic to be addressed, but not between team members.

✦ Outside views are welcome.

✦ Anger and aggressiveness are discouraged.

✦ Team members can be assertive, engage in lively debate, and express contrary views without pressure to "go along" with group consensus. Team members can also disagree without being seen as problematic.

✦ High levels of trust exist.

✦ All team members are encouraged to say what is on their mind, even — perhaps especially — when it is sensitive.

In the sections that follow, a model for effective facilitation is introduced. This model describes and defines the skills or "how-to's" of facilitation. Task, behavior, and climate form the foundation of the model, describing "what" the model is all about. The five skills, or phases, of facilitation provide a simple guide for every facilitation opportunity. Each skill or step explores specific task issues and facilitator behaviors.

The Facilitation Model: The Five Skills

Facilitation is a dynamic, fluid process requiring flexibility from every team member and, more especially, from the facilitator. The five skills of facilitation provide a map to guide facilitators through the process and the tools necessary to effectively facilitate the work of a team.

It is overstating the case to say that facilitation is a simple process. Any interaction that requires the management of diverse interests, needs, and opinions of group members is challenging by nature. In most cases, the performance of the group must also meet certain standards and achieve results defined by the organization, not just the expectations of the team itself. So the balancing act between organizational objectives, the goals of the team, and the desires of individual team members can be a daunting proposition.

Effective facilitation and solid group performance are, however, attainable goals. The process outlined in this book helps facilitators

1. Evaluate and properly prepare for problem-solving situations

2. Gain the support and cooperation of the team

3. Create and implement solid solutions that meet the needs of all stakeholders

4. Diagnose and evaluate personal efforts

The five skills or ingredients of the facilitation process are Engage, Clarify, Deliberate, Act, and Sustain. The longitudinal nature of this process presupposes that the facilitator is not just a "hired gun" brought in to conduct a single meeting. Rather, the steps of this process begin with initial definition and analysis of the task or problem, and end with the implementation of a successful solution. The facilitator plays an important role in every stage of the process.

The model is a free-flowing, cyclical process. Success in each stage helps produce opportunities in another. Careful attention to each phase naturally leads to quality decisions, sound plans, and well-designed projects.

Each completed cycle represents the successful solution to a problem, implementation of a plan, or completion of a project. Each phase provides opportunities to learn from the experience and identifies the next project, task, or challenge to pursue. The process is linear in the sense that it is important to successfully address one stage before moving to the next. However, the process is flexible enough to return to a previous phase when necessary in order to get back on the right course.

> "What we call results are beginnings."
>
> *Ralph Waldo Emerson*

Tips for Team Members

The five skills of facilitation introduced in this chapter provide a road map for facilitating the work of any team or group. Each skill is more fully developed in later sections, whereas this chapter provides an overview of the process.

Look at the Big Picture

✔ To what teams or groups do you belong?

✔ What is your role?

✔ Can you see things that the groups does well, or not so well?

✔ What problems or challenges does your group face?

How Can You Use This Book?

✔ Are you the leader of a group or preparing to be one?

✔ In what areas are you already skilled?

✔ What areas could you improve upon?

CHAPTER 5

Engage

CHAPTER 5

Engage

In the television series *Star Trek: The Next Generation*, Capt. Jean-Luc Picard of the U.S.S. Enterprise frequently instructs his crew to "lay in a course" to their next destination. With the preparations complete, he then utters one word, usually in a highly dramatic fashion, "Engage!"

At this command, Picard's staff presses the buttons that operate the propulsion system of the ship, and the Enterprise leaps forward into space, across thousands of light years, bridging the galaxies. All this power, all this activity and progress, from just one word: Engage!

Wouldn't it be great if it were that easy when facilitating a group? What if all facilitators had to do was just say a single word, or push some high-tech button, and team members would immediately and completely engage? What if team members would connect with each other, understand perfectly what needs to be done, and grasp the direction of the group so easily? Even passing exposure to the facilitation process provides ample evidence that people don't always naturally engage, warm up, or open up automatically.

Why is it so hard to engage the best efforts and best ideas of team members, and then to support, promote, and push forward the best ideas? In many organizations, "The Next Big Thing" has become a running joke, the object of increasing cynicism within the organization. One executive champion or another comes up with a new initiative that will lead the company to profitability and growth. The idea is reviewed at the highest levels and approved. A crack team of devotees then works for months on the all-important launch, which, more often than not, lands with a resounding thud among the rank and file.

How many ideas have been introduced, with fanfare and pyrotechnics, at company gatherings? How many new initiatives have been launched with the figurative "big splash?" And how many of these ideas — some with real merit — have faded into the background as leaders found that, within their teams, they 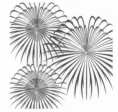 couldn't sustain the enthusiasm and commitment necessary to carry them to their successful conclusion?

The first phase of effective facilitation is to find a way to focus and energize team members, to engage them, and help them find a way to be a part of the solution.

When facilitators can help team members answer the question, "What's In It For Me?" (WIIFM), some excitement for the work can be generated. And if the group can answer the question, "What's In It For Us?," creating a strong, common purpose for the group becomes more of a reality. But if team members can't identify benefits to getting involved in the task or project, nothing will be created except meeting attendance or grudging compliance.

How does a facilitator engage others in the work? What are the "Rules of Engagement?"

Engaging team members isn't a "step" that is accomplished once and never again. Nor is it a series of manipulative techniques to ensure that everyone is "on the same side." Engaging involves a way of being with others, an attitude, an approach that conveys respect, esteem, and value in their contributions.

It has to do with the respect and esteem in which team members hold facilitators as well. In the words of author Stephen R. Covey, leaders must demonstrate that they have both the character and competence necessary to do the job. Both elements are important in becoming the kind of leader that others will willingly follow.

Team members need to feel that their challenges and concerns are understood. They need to see their leaders as knowledgeable and skilled enough to contribute to the problem-solving process in significant ways. Trusting their leader's competence is a component of igniting their energies in the changes, projects, or initiatives decided upon by the group. It is equally important that team members respect their leaders personally, that they see them as people of integrity, worthy of their trust.

In a broad sense, engaging others is an ongoing and long-term proposition requiring consistent skills and beliefs. Some of the effort or tasks required of team members may test the strength of their feelings for their leader, so it is imperative to make a regular effort to build those ties. When the time comes for leaders to ask team members to make a leap of faith and to follow their lead, people assess the credibility and genuine concern their leaders have shown for them and the task. How completely team members engage has a great deal to do with their perceptions of their leader.

> "We are what we repeatedly do; excellence, then, is not an act, but a habit."
>
> *Aristotle*

In regular, day-to-day interaction, engaging others has to do with maintaining a consistent flow of information, acknowledging them and their efforts, and creating a genuine rapport. It requires a demonstration of the leader's enthusiasm, commitment, and optimism. One of the primary areas of effective facilitation is to create a safe environment, where honest feelings can be shared, ideas evaluated, and obstacles addressed. Regardless of position, influence, salary, or connections, each team member must feel comfortable and protected enough to say what's on his/her mind. Team members can sense if it is safe to talk and whether the facilitator wants them to open up and provide ideas. If they pick up signals that their input is not desired, they will generally remain quiet, listen, and be passive, and their leaders will have to work hard to reverse this impression. Once people have retreated to their shell, it is hard to coach them out. It is better to make the effort to ensure that everyone feels needed, welcome, and safe up front.

Much of this process of engaging others, then, comes as a result of relationships built over time, through consistent effort and attention to the needs of individual team members. However, when it's time to actually facilitate a group through a problem-solving or planning session, there are additional actions, behaviors, and attitudes that can ensure success.

At the beginning of a facilitation meeting or interaction, greet and acknowledge each member. Get to know new members, find something out about them, and remember their names. Be friendly, open, and enthusiastic, setting a positive, optimistic tone for the work to be done. Even if the topic to be addressed is serious, a creative, inclusive atmosphere is established by the way the meeting begins.

Ground Rules

It's important to review the group's ground rules in the beginning. The best results are generated when each team member feels free and safe to say whatever needs to be said, without worrying that it will be perceived in a negative way. Again, the leader's previous track record and experience with the group will either help or hinder. If team members have high trust and largely positive experiences in previous interactions with you, they'll be more likely to open up and really contribute to the dialogue. If, on the other hand, they live in an environment of low trust, or have had negative consequences from speaking up in the past, it will require more effort and patience to draw them out and encourage them to contribute.

Engage the Group

Here are a few more practical "how-to's" on effectively engaging team members in a group discussion:

+ Occasionally use a warm-up activity, present a brainteaser, or share a favorite quote or idea to ignite interaction and to get the group thinking.

+ Review the role of a facilitator: to observe; to introduce ideas, topics, or challenges; to manage (but not control) the group's interactions; to maintain ground rules; and to help guide the group to a solution or conclusion.

+ Begin asking questions as soon as possible; get people talking about expectations; help them agree upon the ground rules and goals for the group.

+ Recognize team member contributions by recording or documenting their contributions in a visible way (flip charts, white boards, etc.).

+ Reinforce applicable confidentiality guidelines.

+ Establish a "safe environment" by asking team members to leave titles, positions, and other agendas behind, and to commit to contributing to discussions and solutions.

+ Reinforce and thank "early" contributors, those brave enough to start the discussion or raise points.

+ Gently draw out team members by using broad questions that they can jump on.

+ Demonstrate active listening; restate and clarify points; summarize when appropriate.

+ Connect non-verbally; use open body postures, gestures, and eye contact; move around and move in close when appropriate to capture ideas and attention.

+ Keep the conversation balanced between the dominant extroverts and the reserved introverts.

+ Create breaks and ways for people to move around, divide into sub-groups, and do something physical.

Engage Obstacles

Watch out for some common obstacles and challenges that arise throughout the discussion:

+ Some team members may complain about the composition of

the group or their assignment. It's important to listen and understand, because these may be rooted in a valid concern.

✦ Some team members may express suspicion about the process, their selection to the problem-solving team, or even the facilitator.

> "Wise men have long ears, big eyes, and a short tongue."
>
> *Anonymous*

✦ Some team members may be too vocal and dominating, while others may be too passive or may wonder when or if they will have a chance to contribute.

✦ Some confident and independent team members may consider this kind of group interaction a waste of time, claiming that they have too much work to do to spend time in another meaningless meeting.

A facilitator may feel challenged, threatened, intimidated, or nervous at the prospect of having to lead a demanding or tough group, with its varying issues, agendas, and personalities, through the sometimes difficult and tense process of discussion, debate, problem-solving, and reaching a consensus. A facilitator may focus more on arriving at a solution than on the process of getting there by becoming impatient and pushing too hard or too fast to achieve real group synergy. All of these dynamics threaten the work of the group today and its ability to address similar issues in the future. As a facilitator, it takes time, patience, an open mind, and the courage to own up to mistakes and correct them to effectively lead a group.

Facilitator Behaviors

It takes a unique combination of self-confidence and trust in team members and the facilitation process to help groups reach solutions. A facilitator needs confidence in his/her own abilities and agenda, and to trust the abilities of others to collaborate creatively. Here are some additional tools that will increase a facilitator's confidence in dealing with the challenges inherent in facilitating the work of a team:

✦ Actively listening to what the group has to say may be the single most important factor in successfully facilitating a meeting. Some facilitators have perfected the thoughtful gaze, giving the impression of listening, while actually composing the next wise or pithy remark. It requires real attention and concern to maintain a genuine listening posture, and it is critical that team members never have reason to suspect that they are not being heard.

✦ If a facilitator doesn't understand, or disagrees with what is being said, ask for clarification, more information, and other perspectives from the group. Resist the temptation to rush to judgment, to provide an opinion, or to respond directly to everything that is said. Let the contributions come from team members, spontaneously and naturally. Uncomfortable topics or comments generally need to be raised and expressed. The benefits of establishing an open dialogue far outweigh the risks of having conflicting or dissenting views thrown around. When team members see openness, non-defensiveness, and an ability to withhold judgment on the part of the facilitator, they are more likely to mimic this behavior.

✦ Team members' comments can be captured by writing them down on a white board or flipchart. This, too, conveys a spirit of openness and objectivity in hearing and dealing with everything that is said. It isn't necessary to spend time on every idea that is raised. In fact, one of the more important roles of the facilitator is to help the group choose relevant topics to address during that specific meeting. But if each idea is given attention by writing it down (and perhaps identifying another time to address it), team members will feel included and respected.

✦ After the initial feelings and perceptions of the group are captured, it is time to "chalk the field" for the meeting. Remind the group of its goal or purpose. What does the group need to achieve? What tasks does the

group need to accomplish? What results will it need to eventually deliver?

✦ Whether the task is assigned by someone else or defined during the group discussion, at some point it will be important to reduce it to a manageable framework. This may require setting some topics aside for later discussion. It's important to have a clear focus for the facilitation, so that you and the group can see when it's getting off track and maintain a focus on the topic at hand.

✦ Actively enforce the ground rules. Refer to Chapter 14: Establishing Ground Rules, and make them a dynamic and "living" document. Keep the ground rules as simple as possible, and help team members focus on and come to open agreement about how they will:

> "Effective communication is 20% what you know, and 80% how you feel about what you know."
>
> *Jim Rohn*

1. Communicate with one another.

2. Respond to the ideas of others.

3. Contribute to both the conversation and the subsequent tasks and responsibilities that may come from the discussion.

✦ As a facilitator, consider your own personal style and how it might contribute to or detract from the success of the facilitation. Here are some questions to consider:

1. Am I a "driver," compelled to accomplish the task at hand?

2. Do I generally listen well, gather data, and involve others in the decisions I have to make?

3. Am I inclusive and collaborative by nature, or more directive?

Understanding personal tendencies helps facilitators manage the flow of the group's progress and make adjustments as necessary. Frustrated by seemingly endless discussion, a facilitator may naturally move into a directive role.

A facilitator may also get caught up in the creative comments and ideas, and fail to converge on the goal. Both the interaction and the end result are important, and the facilitator walks a fine line in achieving success in both. Keep the following ideas in mind to engage team members:

1. Use positive language, encouraging team members to elaborate or expand upon ideas. Ensure responses are evenly distributed. Use comments like these:

   ✦ "Thanks for sharing your ideas."

   ✦ "That's a good point. Are there any other thoughts?"

   ✦ "Keep going. We are making good progress."

   ✦ "Can you expand on that idea?"

2. Listen actively, using summaries and questions to clarify key points for the group:

   ✦ "Bob, here's what I think you just said…(summarize the point, then ask)…Is that an accurate assessment?"

   ✦ "Does this need further discussion, or is the group ready for a break?"

   ✦ "Can somebody else summarize what Sherrie just said?"

3. Take ownership for mistakes and missteps along the way:

   ✦ "That was my mistake. I'm sorry — I didn't realize that you had more you wanted to say on this."

   ✦ "I apologize. I think I may have cut someone off on this side of the room."

   ✦ "I forgot to come back to you, Kim. Do you still want to share an idea?"

The ultimate goal in this phase of facilitation is to help the team members be as comfortable as possible. Be relaxed, and observe the mood of the group. Are team members committed, or do they feel like prisoners and victims? Get to know team members individually. Express positive feelings of being with them and working on the task. Be friendly and inclusive, acknowledging their requests and needs. A facilitator is the "trustee" for the group. A facilitator needs to demonstrate and promote respect, and to drive out fears. Good facilitators are active, passionate, and upbeat. They demonstrate that they want to be with the group. They are willing to be neutral, yet expose their values and connect with the team in a positive, beneficial manner.

Engaging the group means harnessing their best energies for the task. Team members are engaged when they sit up straighter, attend to the discussion, offer spontaneous, rapid-fire suggestions, build on and respond positively to what others say, and even begin side conversations about an idea they can't wait to share. With their collective effort and contribution, just about any problem can be solved, any project executed, any situation resolved.

Checklist for Facilitators

Use this checklist to ensure that you are fully engaging your group.

Climate and Behaviors

✦ Be responsible and demonstrate your acceptance of others.

✦ Own up to problems and oversights if they occur.

✦ Describe your expectations for a safe, two-way communication environment.

✦ Defend all contributors; encourage participants to relax and open up.

✦ Promptly manage interruptions, encroachments, and members "talking over" each other.

✦ Ask members to summarize what others say to promote understanding.

✦ Ask probing questions (reflect, connect, project).

✦ Alter the pace; create physical and mental breaks.

✦ Expose your own humor, and enable others to express humor as well (light humor vs. entertain).

✦ Expound on unexpected or spontaneous humor or fun situations.

✦ Be willing to laugh at yourself and not be serious all of the time.

Connect to Group Members

✦ Help the group become comfortable with you; interact with each person and call him/her by name.

✦ Describe your feelings and emotions toward the group and the task — be authentic.

✦ Model "active listening" skills.

✦ Support, encourage, and reinforce those who are less vocal.

✦ Use non-verbals: move around (sit and stand), use gestures, expressions, and visuals.

✦ Demonstrate and express your enthusiasm.

✦ Be upbeat and positive.

✦ Use "easy" eye contact.

✦ Be attentive and focused — show that you want to be there.

Procedures and Practices

✦ Express your neutrality and describe your role.

✦ Establish ground rules, norms, and behavioral expectations (the contract).

✦ Develop procedural strategies and methods to handle decisions, conflicts, etc.

✦ Create sub-groups for discussion.

✦ Control boundaries for humor (good taste, amount, and type).

Tips for Team Members

"Engage" means to get connected to something, to get excited about it, and to get involved. Your team will only be as successful as you, and the other individual members, make it. What can you do to get "engaged" in the work of your team?

Make Sure You Understand Your Team's Goals, Mission, and Purpose

✔ Do you know what your team is trying to achieve this year? This quarter? This month? This week?

✔ Talk to your team leaders. Ask questions. Learn what's important to them. What are their big issues?

Evaluate Your Contribution

✔ What kind of an attitude do you bring to the work of your team?

✔ Do you participate fully in team discussions?

✔ Do you bring your best ideas, energies, and cooperation to team projects?

✔ What else could you do to help your team succeed?

Develop Yourself

✔ In what areas could you develop skills and capabilities that will help your team succeed?

✔ Talk with your team leader or manager about a personal development plan.

✔ Research additional training, education, or work experiences that could increase your value to the organization.

CHAPTER 6

Clarify

CHAPTER 6
Clarify

Engaging the team in the work is a critical component of success. Engaging is both a skill and a "way of being." Most of the relationship and rapport building that effective facilitation requires is a feature of ongoing interaction with the team. Like farmers, effective facilitators have to "sow the seeds" long before the harvest.

Therefore, a major "task" of the facilitation process is to clarify what the team needs to achieve. This process is also referred to as "framing" or "focusing" on the task or project at hand. One of the greatest challenges with most teams is that they have so many issues to deal with. It can be difficult to identify and set aside lower priorities, and then properly define the scope and focus on the central objective to be achieved.

It takes some discipline from both the facilitator and the team members to address only the "main" topic during a discussion. People are social animals; we all like to visit, and it is easy for groups to get distracted. People like to show off their expertise, and some people feel a need to elaborate on and over-analyze every angle of the discussion. One very common occurrence is to start dealing with one topic and then get distracted by any number of secondary issues that arise in the course of the discussion. One of the facilitator's most important roles is to help the group define the scope and shape of the task or topic, and then to maintain a clear focus on resolving that issue, launching that project, or resolving that problem.

One of our clients uses a powerful but effective strategy for the

"Clarify" phase of facilitation. This method involves laying the foundation for a discussion by spending a few brief moments on three points: purpose, process, and payoff. Leading the group through a discussion of the three points clarifies the questions that most people have when they enter a discussion:

+ **Purpose:** Why are we here? What is the desired result?

+ **Process:** How are we going to work/operate together to achieve our need?

+ **Payoff:** What is the intended benefit?

Answers to these questions should be vigorously discussed and defined. They should be documented and made visible. Unless the team has a pre-defined or set mission, we all have our own ideas of the purpose, process, and payoff. Once the brainstorming is complete, a facilitator needs to help the group prioritize, combine, and converge on a realistic "clarification" statement. The following questions are helpful:

> Unless the team has a pre-defined or set mission, we all have our own ideas of the purpose, process, and payoff.

Purpose

+ "What is the number one goal?"

+ "Can someone describe a specific objective for this group?"

+ "What does success look like in your mind?"

+ "Who is our customer?"

+ "What do you think our product or deliverable is?"

+ "What does a successful experience look like for you?"

Process

+ "How do you think we should go about this task or mission?"

+ "What is our plan of attack to achieve our objectives?"

+ "What is the sequence of tasks/agenda?"

+ "What approach, techniques, or skills will help us reach our target goals?"

+ "Is there a process that we can use today to move forward?"

Payoff

+ "How will our work benefit you (and us)?"

+ "What will be most beneficial for our customers when we complete this discussion?"

+ "How will others use or apply what we come up with?"

+ "Where will our work ultimately lead?"

It may be helpful to record the "side issues" that arise on a flipchart or white board. This is sometimes referred to as a "parking  lot" of secondary issues. Many side issues are genuine, valid, and deserving of consideration, but they are separate questions that ought to be addressed at another time. Maintaining focus may require establishing specific time to address and resolve certain issues in the parking lot. A desire to deal with these issues at another time needs to be clearly communicated, so that team members can be assured that their issues are not being ignored.

One process that began in the "Engage" phase needs to be further pursued at this point. At the beginning of any facilitation, it's important to review ground rules for interaction to ensure open, positive communication and contributions by team members. In the "Clarify" stage, that process is extended to define and come to agreement on some of the following information:

+ Behavioral ground rules; how team members will interact with one another.

+ Expectations of team members, leaders, and facilitators.

+ The processes and procedures the group will follow to arrive at its conclusions.

✦ Final decision-making authority in case of an impasse.

✦ The group's over-arching purpose, mission, task, and scope as they relate to this interaction.

✦ Who the customers or stakeholders are for the project.

✦ The deliverables — a plan, agenda, or decision — that the group is charged with creating.

Facilitators first need to help the group establish ground rules and guiding principles. This task is easier if the team has already established principles of mutual respect, a positive attitude, open communication, and trust. It can be more difficult if the team has developed a dysfunctional pattern of destructive communication, political intrigue, or mistrust, or if some members have hidden agendas or a "me first" mentality.

"High expectations are the key to everything"

Sam Walton

There is an old coaching bromide that states, "There is no 'I' in team." But it's important to notice that there is an "m" and an "e" ("ME!") in "team," and some team members are keenly aware of and committed to the benefits they might receive by making themselves look good, regardless of the impact on the rest of the team. A facilitator should consider the following questions in determining how prepared the team is to work together as a unit to achieve group objectives:

✦ Do team members see the team as centrally important?

✦ Have they experienced positive interaction and synergy in the past?

✦ Is there a lack of trust?

✦ How do they feel about you as a leader or facilitator?

Checklist for Facilitators

Use the following checklist to ensure that you are successfully clarifying the topic, task, or issue at hand:

Purpose

✦ Distill written purpose statements. What does success look like?

✦ Why is the group meeting? What is the task?

✦ Probe and follow up by asking others to build, bridge, or link ideas or information.

✦ "Direction" — Focus the group on the topics, problems, and issues. Watch out for diversions.

✦ "Depth" — Challenge the group; avoid over-analysis (perfection) or under-analysis (shallowness).

Process

✦ Jointly define the agenda, topics, and timetable.

✦ Visually capture all ideas, and document both facts and opinions.

✦ Encourage brainstorming and innovation vs. critiquing.

✦ Help the group select and use appropriate tools, techniques, and applications.

✦ Encourage openness, sharing, diversity, and flexible thinking.

✦ Promote discovery, reflection, and insight.

✦ Embrace and reward creativity, spontaneity, and inspiration.

✦ Encourage synergy.

✦ Move from "easy," open-ended questions to more challenging and deeper questions.

✦ Balance the interaction opportunities. Draw out input from all participants (call on members, and give everyone a voice).

✦ Verbally reinforce participation efforts.

✦ Respond to feedback and suggestions from team members.

✦ "Speed" — Keep the group moving; reference the clock. Keep the timetable and agenda in sync.

✦ Control tangents and keep the group on track — "Park" miscellaneous issues.

✦ Explore alternatives if time runs short.

Payoff

✦ What are the desired outcomes?

✦ What will this group produce/deliver?

Tips for Team Members

"Clarify" means taking the responsibility to ensure that everyone is clear about the goal of the task or project. Unclear communication is perhaps the biggest obstacle to effectiveness and success in teams. Clarify also means understanding roles, responsibilities, and commitments to contribute.

Make Sure You Understand Your Team's Ground Rules and Procedures

✔ How do things work in your team? How are you expected to operate in order to get things done?

✔ Do you contribute to the effective operation of your team by abiding by the accepted norms and rules?

✔ Do you fully listen to other team members and the facilitator? Do you avoid judging and making assumptions?

Ask Questions

✔ Do you ask questions when you're not clear about a task or assignment?

✔ Are you comfortable with approaching your facilitator for help or more understanding?

Know Your Role

✔ Do you know what your facilitator expects from you?

✔ Do you know what other team members expect from you?

✔ Are you clear about your level of empowerment on various tasks?

Support Your Team

✔ How do you treat other team members?

✔ Are you cooperative and willing to help them?

✔ Do you speak with them, and about them, with respect?

CHAPTER 7

Deliberate

Deliberate

Some people might argue that "Deliberate" is the most important element in the facilitation process. Whether that is true for your group or not, this stage is vitally important because it is where the group's talents, insights, wisdom, and knowledge are really applied to the task. Whether the mission is problem solving, decision making, planning, studying, negotiating, or creating, groups have to successfully negotiate through the process of deliberation, discussion, consideration, and debate.

Deliberation builds upon the "Clarify" stage by asking the team to more deeply explore the challenge, gather data, discuss options, and choose a course of action. The facilitator helps the team locate accurate information, think creatively, ensure that each relevant perspective is heard, and assess the pros and cons of every point of view. With this preparation, the team can settle on the facts and ultimately create a workable solution.

An important cautionary note for the facilitator is that leaders frequently feel obliged to be the source of all answers and wisdom. Leaders or facilitators may feel responsible to make all the decisions, create the entire solution, and include all the "bells and whistles" in order to substantiate their worthiness to lead.

Furthermore, leaders are usually given early insights into the problems, challenges, or opportunities their team has to face, which can contribute to this feeling of responsibility. The leader may also

have time to brainstorm solutions or even create a plan ahead of time to present to the team. But leaders who "pre-form" the solution before the team even hears that there is a problem, rob both the leader and team members of a valuable opportunity to tap into the synergy and power of the group. Many leaders simply are not comfortable and secure enough to allow the best ideas and plans to emerge from the storehouse of talent and experience within their teams.

Some leaders may struggle with trust and delegation because they feel they can see what needs to be done and implement it in less time than they can explain it to someone else. In some cases, they might be able to create the best solution while team members are still trying to grasp the problem at hand. But these approaches don't generate growth and development among team members, let alone help the team discover and create powerful solutions to daily challenges and demands.

> "All that is valuable in human society depends upon the opportunity for development accorded the individual."
>
> *Albert Einstein*

There are actually two parts to the deliberation process: diverging and converging. Diverging means that the group is engaged in an open, free-flowing discussion. The group could be brainstorming, exploring, sharing, or dumping out information. Converging, on the other hand, means closing in, choosing, concluding, taking a position, or reaching an understanding. For facilitators and team members alike, diverging and converging are two very different pieces of work. However, both parts can be dynamic and exciting for the facilitator and the group.

For a skilled facilitator, the "Deliberate" phase is about gathering the information, tools, and resources necessary to allow the team to fully understand the problem, and then create the best possible solution, drawing from the team's collective strengths, knowledge, and experiences.

Part One: Diverge

Diverging is helping the group review the data, probe deeper, and have a rich and open discussion about the topic. The facilitator's role is to guide the group as it breaks down and examines the issues. Facilitators invite the group to contribute facts and data by asking open-ended questions, clarifying and redirecting responses, and directly probing team members. The purpose of collecting and analyzing data is to keep groups from jumping to a decision or action before the issue has thoroughly been examined and debated.

One problem many facilitators struggle with during the diverging phase is dealing effectively with conflict. Groups sometimes fall victim to the false notion that productive groups are always harmonious. The truth is, too much harmony, or too little conflict, can keep a group from reaching its full potential. Conflict actually stimulates creativity and pushes the group to new heights. In order for conflict to be productive, however, the facilitator must channel the tension and conflict, and not let it boil over or escalate into personal attacks.

Facilitators sometimes start to panic when discord and differences arise. They often rush in and try to rescue the group by calming the agitators. In actuality, agitators play a critical role during the first part of deliberation by being willing to "stir the pot," take risks, and challenge conventional wisdom. The key is for the facilitator to create a safe place for the group to challenge each other within the boundaries of constructive tension. Establish ground rules for stimulating diverse ideas — don't allow the discussion to become ugly or allow team members to attack each other's character, personality, or uniqueness. Establishing a climate of tolerance for different views, experiences, and interpretations of the data creates a safe environment for team members to deliberate or openly say what is on their mind.

One organization that we work with likes to refer to this phenomenon as "creative abrasion." In other words, innovation demands divergence more than conformity or cohesiveness. The facilitator regulates the deliberation and intervenes so that the group doesn't "come apart at the seams." Facilitators have to prevent premature compro-

mise as a response to interpersonal conflict. Observant facilitators balance the influence of high-status members who often feel that they have a permission slip to dominate the discussion or direct its course, while lower-status members often keep to themselves. Facilitators must draw out the best contributions of all team members.

> If your group can handle conflict constructively, your group has evolved.

Conflict can occur in several stages of a group's life cycle. However, in deliberation, conflict is uniquely valuable. If groups are going to move to higher levels of performance and in new directions, then old paradigms have to be broken. As a professor once said, "The group that fights together, stays together." In fact, when group members successfully navigate through differences, they gain higher levels of ownership for the group's products, striving harder for solutions, and thinking more critically. Managing conflict successfully builds both confidence and cohesion, while avoiding the nasty side affects of collusion.

> I may disagree with what you say, but I will defend to the death your right to say it.

Remember, at this stage the group should be dealing more with substantive conflict (content), not emotional clashes between individuals. Interpersonal conflict should be sorted out earlier in the "Engage" and "Clarify" stages of facilitation.

Part Two: Converge

As the group process evolves and differences are reconciled, it becomes increasingly unproductive to revert to opposing positions. Simply put, there is a time to disagree and debate, and there is a time to collaborate and consent. As a facilitator, you need to help people on and off the "conflict train." After the period of divergence and deviance, facilitators should guide the group through objective analysis by finding common themes, reviewing the facts, letting go of "pet" preferences, and rendering a group-based verdict.

Quality collaborative efforts demand debate and rigorous examination of the issues. Ideas, information, and opinions that surface in the deliberate phase are thrown into the discussion pool and form the raw material of a group's final consensus.

> "Better bend than break."
>
> *Scottish Proverb*

Converging is drastically different than diverging. Successful group facilitation is a blend of influence, persuasion, compromise, negotiation, argumentation, flexibility, and consensus. As the group turns the corner and "converges," the team has to make sense of and digest the ideas, concerns, and information that emerged in the diverging part of deliberation. Facilitators can then help the group converge by:

+ Distilling

+ Shifting

+ Sorting

+ Screening

+ Evaluating

+ Rating

+ Ranking

+ Deciding

These actions may come naturally to team members who have a bottom line, "make it happen" type of personality. For others in the group, the shift from "Diverging" to "Converging" can be an abrupt shock to their creative or intuitive style.

As the group moves to "Converge," facilitators must remind the group of the mission or target established in the "Clarify" stage. If the mission is to decide, recommend, choose, and conclude, then the group should be led to closure at this point.

Ground rules should define how decisions are made: by consensus, sub-committee, vote, or at the leader's discretion. Whatever the agreed-upon process, team members ultimately face that final task — to settle on a plan, detail it, and successfully implement it.

Here, the facilitator wraps up the "Converging" process and be-

gins to set the stage for the action planning discussion. It may require a direct statement such as:

✦ "In the next five minutes, I want to shut down the brainstorming and debate and begin to consolidate and evaluate our options and analysis."

✦ "It is time to move on. Does anyone have a final creative thought before we move on?"

Facilitators should be prepared to offer some structure for the "Converging" discussion to help the group link ideas, summarize, and conclude. The use of problem-solving and decision-making tools allows the group to capitalize on its creative work. The facilitator then helps the group develop decision criteria and evaluate alternatives, do a root cause analysis, prioritize ideas, or build flow charts. As the group formulates findings, conclusions, and shared understanding, it is time to test consensus. Ask the group if they approve of the picture that is emerging. Some people may find the closure very uncomfortable. Remind the group that the decision isn't necessarily set in stone. Rather, it is a work in progress. If the conclusions don't look right, then the group should circle back to the first part of the "Deliberate" phase and gather new information. However, just because a group doesn't like the look of the final decision doesn't necessarily make it wrong.

If objectives and guidelines are clear to all team members, thinking and choosing becomes an exciting process. With a little observation, it is simple to identify the type of group that is likely to "jump-to-conclusions," the type that wants to discuss every detail and alternative to death, or somewhere in-between.

Sometimes teams get caught up in feeling that they must reach unanimity in order to succeed. Unanimity is tough; it may be impossible to please everyone with a given plan. Consensus, on the other hand, may not represent a perfect agreement. However, consensus means that the group has general agreement and has decided on a course of action that everyone can support.

"Task" vs. "Relationship"

One of the most important responsibilities of a facilitator is to strike a balance between "task" and "relationship." While the group's output and results are critical, it's equally important to build the group and develop their capacity and strength for the future. It can be challenging to find that line — to spend the right amount of time in deliberation, and to ensure that all team members feel included and involved. In the "Deliberate" stage, the balance between "task" and "relationship" responsibilities is really tested. Some hard-charging teams want to get to the solution as quickly as possible, valuing results above dialogue. A case can be made for this focus; in fact, performance is a critical commitment that high-performing teams make. But leaders and team members alike must also consider individual needs and development. Learning how to reach good solutions is just as important as results. In the end, teams will continue to grow only if they learn to draw out the best contributions of each member and expand their capacity.

> "You cannot teach a man anything; you can only help him find it within himself."
>
> *Galileo*

Checklist for Facilitators

+ Test the group's willingness to decide or act (watch for approach-avoidance behavior).

+ Search for final options and preferences.

+ Define standards and criteria for the solution.

+ Lead the group through a decision process, and reinforce consensus guidelines.

+ Clarify the test assumptions and theories — reality vs. perception.

+ Apply the principles of consensus, and build ownership.

+ Look for group dysfunction (conflict, tension, silence, nit-picking, "group think," etc.) that needs to be surfaced.

+ Call "time out;" stop the work on a task when there is a process issue or a dysfunction.

+ "Observe it" — Notice the pattern and repetition of the problem.

+ "Name it" — Call it out, and name the behavior (neutral, non-punishing description) that is creating a problem.

+ "Silence" — Promote reflection and insight; let the tension rise.

+ "Guide" — Allow the group to "own" (or deny) the problem.

Tips for Team Members

"Deliberate" involves all the processes of determining how the team (or individual team members) will go about defining, interpreting, and accomplishing their goals. Groups first "Diverge" to capture diverse viewpoints, and then "Converge" to a clear focus. The resultant plan identifies what will be done, how it will be done, and what the approach to addressing possible obstacles will be.

Participate in Creating the Solution

✦ Do you get involved appropriately in helping your team create plans, or do you hang back, waiting for someone else to take the lead?

✦ Do you jump in when you have something to contribute, such as a new idea, previous experience, or success with an issue?

Think Creatively

✦ Set time aside on a regular basis to consider the challenges your team is facing, and explore ideas you can take to your leaders or manager.

✦ Evaluate your areas of responsibility: Are there improvements that ought to be made to processes or practices?

Get Behind the Plan

✦ Help your team stay on task during meetings and discussions; focus on solutions.

✦ Raise concerns and issues during the process to ensure that all pertinent information is heard and considered.

✦ When a decision is reached by the team, commit yourself to helping the team succeed.

CHAPTER 8

Act

CHAPTER 8
Act

Traditional history teaches that Christopher Columbus, sailing under the provenance of the Queen of Spain, was planning to find a trade route to China when he stumbled upon the New World. By most accounts, he didn't realize just what he'd found until later, but he was quick to see the possibilities for growth and enrichment.

Whatever his intent, Columbus learned quickly what all good facilitators find out sooner or later: The best-laid plans take unexpected turns, and leadership has more to do with managing uncertainty and change than with creating a certain road map for success.

As a facilitator, have you ever conducted what you thought was a successful planning discussion, assigned tasks and projects, and adjourned, confident that team members were focused, clear, and committed? Then, a few weeks later, as critical dates and deadlines approached, did you find that little or no progress had been made? Have you adjourned meetings under the assumption that consensus had been built and that team members understood expectations, only to find out later that there were different viewpoints?

So how can facilitators ensure that plans turn into successful projects? How does effective facilitation transfer into the kinds of business results for which the facilitator and team members can feel justifiably proud and receive recognition?

The hard fact is that there is no simple formula, no "Shazam!" that automatically ensures success. There are, however, a few practices that help maintain the dynamic excitement and creativity of a successful discussion, as team members go about the hard work of putting in place what has been planned or decided.

> "He who would leap must take a long run"
>
> *Danish Proverb*

The "Act" phase for a skilled facilitator is about creating the best possible action plan by drawing from team members' collective strengths, knowledge, and experience. There's a fine line between preparing the team to create a plan and allowing the team to create a plan of its own.

Planning builds upon the "Deliberate" stage by asking the team to marshal its resources and then create a sustainable and complete plan to act on. A few souls out there consistently succeed in delivering results. A few groups always make good on promised deadlines. A few facilitators develop reputations as the "can-do" people to whom the organization turns when important tasks must be done. The key to successful implementation of the plan is twofold:

+ Delegate action items effectively.

+ Create a climate where every team member accepts personal accountability.

These simple steps are used by every successful facilitator. They're easy to remember, but frequently much more difficult for both facilitators and team members to mold into habits.

Delegation

The problems with delegation can be found along a continuum. At one end are the facilitators who can't let go. Perhaps they haven't developed trust in a new or inexperienced group and aren't comfortable letting individual team members run with the ball. Perhaps they are inflexible, worry about letting go of control, or just don't think anyone else can do it as well as they can. Whatever the reason, these facilitators find themselves overwhelmed by a myriad of tasks, frequently behind schedule, and leading an under-utilized group that may never develop the capacities required to take on significant projects.

At the other end of the spectrum are facilitators who dump projects and tasks on unprepared or underdeveloped team members, without providing the information, instruction, or resources necessary for success. They may be "big picture" leaders, not wanting to be  troubled by details. They may also be so busy with other projects that they adopt a "sink-or-swim" attitude toward team members. While a few team members may rise to the occasion through initiative or previous experience, many team members feel abandoned, insecure, and frustrated because they want to do well but are simply unprepared and inadequately provided for.

Some facilitators in the middle of the continuum generally want team members to accept responsibility and give them the tools needed to succeed, but they fall short in the way responsibilities are delegated. The greatest enemy of delegation is lack of clarity. Opportunities and deadlines are often missed because of a misunderstanding. Perhaps one team member thought someone else was responsible or thought that the deadline was next week, not this week.

Accountability

The second step to implementation is creating an accountable culture. This is one of the first and most important responsibilities of the facilitator. Team members respond in a positive and proactive way when they see those at the top taking responsibility, living up to commitments, and connecting positively with others.

To ensure every task is effectively delegated, the facilitator and the responsible team member need to acknowledge it verbally and, if possible, record it in some fashion (electronically, in written form, etc.). Some groups do this routinely, while others see it as an unnecessary formality. Regardless, groups that record and recognize each commitment in this way have a much greater record of success.

Facilitators who simply assign tasks risk the team member not hearing, understanding, or being willing to commit. Fortunately, it's a simple process to reverse. Instead of reciting tasks and assignments, ask team members to summarize and re-state plans and commitments. As a colleague says, "When I say it, it's just words. When they say it, it's a commitment."

Recording tasks provides an extra measure of security and a helpful framework for follow-up meetings. If a question arises, the record provides a clarifying check on both the timelines and responsibilities. This isn't meant to embarrass team members, but it doesn't take many of these experiences for facilitators and team members alike to recognize the accountable culture in which they are living, and to respond accordingly.

There should never be a commitment asked for or made for which the team member is not eventually held accountable. Failing to follow up, or letting things slide, sends a clear message that it doesn't really matter whether team members do what they've committed to or not.

On the other hand, when team members see the facilitator's commitment to the process and willingness to be responsible for promises, they generally respond in a positive manner. Some team

> "Example is not the main thing in influencing others — it's the only thing."
>
> *Albert Schweitzer*

members may do it grudgingly at first, but once they know the rules, and that everyone has to play by them, they'll appreciate the opportunities for growth that true accountability provides.

Acting on plans is too often a neglected step, but it's the key to translating ideas into real results. This is where the rubber meets the road. Groups build momentum through effectively planning and then successfully implementing projects and tasks.

Checklist for Facilitators

Use the following checklist to ensure that you are effectively planning, implementing, and taking action that will bring about the success of your project.

✦ Confirm agreement by asking everyone to express his/her commitment level.

✦ Check for and note reservations, concerns, and fears.

✦ Discuss options, prevention, or contingencies.

✦ Create shared ownership and personal choice; test the support level for action.

✦ Close out the discussion by reviewing understandings, agreements, and resolutions.

✦ Clarify commitments, actions, assignments, and responsibilities.

✦ Confirm time frames and mileposts.

✦ Measure the action plans against the SMART criteria. Are the plans **S**pecific, **M**easurable, **A**ction-Oriented, **R**ealistic, and **T**ime-bound?

Tips for Team Members

"Act" involves all the processes of determining how the team (or individual team members) will go about accomplishing its goals. The action plan identifies what will be done, how it will be done, and what the approach to addressing possible obstacles will be.

Following Through on Commitments

✔ What have you agreed to do? Are you clear on what, when, where, why?

✔ Record your commitments; create an accountable timeline for their completion.

✔ Report back at agreed-upon times; don't make them come looking for you. Communication is the key.

What to Do When Things Go Wrong

✔ Don't wait until it's too late. Talk to someone as soon as you can see it's going to affect others.

✔ Take responsibility: both for the things that you may have missed, and for helping to resolve them. Own up.

CHAPTER 9

Sustain

Sustain

The final skill of effective facilitation is so rarely practiced that many organizations have a hard time recognizing it as part of the facilitation process. There are two key pieces to the "Sustain" process:

✦ Follow-up

✦ Evaluation

Follow-up

It's been said that everyone could be great, if the world was only watching for a moment. It's much more difficult to maintain great effort over time, especially through the inevitable tough times, and that  is when most projects fail. Day-to-day pressures, distractions, and dilemmas frequently submarine the commitments that team members make. Some people overestimate their ability or capacity or have fuzzy priorities, and most people feel they simply have too much to do or are not fully on board with the plan of action. Many facilitators assume that their job is complete when comprehensive and detailed assignments, tasks, and plans are created. But time and time again, once discussions are complete, things go wrong, due to unclear communication, incomplete follow-up, or changing conditions. Success is measured not in how smoothly meetings are conducted, but in how well team members support decisions and execute plans after the meeting.

Follow-up isn't a complex process, but it takes consistency and commitment. There are a number of ways to effectively follow up on assignments: send an e-mail (particularly one that requires the team member to read and respond), drop by an office to check in, or catch someone in the hallway to ask a question. More complex projects usually require regularly scheduled meetings, planned at frequent-enough intervals to ensure that the team is moving forward at an appropriate pace, to react to changing conditions that may require changes to the plan, and to publicize progress and successes.

The accountability process in follow-up meetings should be the same as in the initial action planning. Team members should be given the opportunity to report on their stewardships, as well as to raise concerns, questions, or problems, and to make further commitments regarding what they will do next. The culture should be one where everyone is more committed to solutions than to blame. The facilitator may have to do little more than keep the group on schedule and follow the agenda.

A facilitator focused on sustainable solutions ensures that the organization's processes and systems support team members as they go about implementing solutions and acting on the agreed upon plans. Most importantly, facilitators recognize and reward the progress and successes of team members. This is a vital component of sustaining the group effort. Leaders who are great facilitators think about the sustainability process and are focused on strategies for leading groups to sustained solutions.

> "Strategy is when you run out of ammunition, but keep fighting anyway."
>
> *Norman Vincent Peale*

Evaluation

Many groups are so grateful to finally finish projects and tasks and move on to the next ones, that team members fail to recognize what can be learned from the results. Certainly, some groups reward and celebrate the successful conclusion of projects, but even that is not as common a practice as it should be. And when a project is something less than successful, most groups try to defend their work, bury it publicly, and forget it as quickly as possible. But the examination of the results, both positive and negative, is among the greatest opportunities for growth and learning.

How many facilitators make a practice of evaluating and debriefing personal and team member efforts? How many facilitators are willing to expose and scrutinize, for better or worse, the relative effectiveness of the last assignment? How many groups have enough of a secure and trusting foundation to allow for open, honest, and candid examination both of what went well and of what needs improvement?

In one leading consulting firm, a new CEO asked associates to create a list entitled, "The Dumb Things We Do." Over the history of the firm, various practices had sprung up which might have had some relevance at one point, but were found to be unnecessary, wasteful, counterproductive, and maybe just plain dumb. The lists were collected and evaluated, and changes were made to several procedures that resulted in cost savings of over $40 million in the first two years.

Consider the statistics kept by most professional, college, high school, and even some little league baseball teams. Detailed, accurate records are kept of earned runs allowed by pitchers, batting averages of every player on the team, and even such arcane minutiae as the tendencies of a certain left-handed pitcher against a power-hitting team.

Professional sports franchises employ an army of scouts, statisticians, and coaches who break down videotape, calculate the numerical representations of performance, and create detailed strategies for almost every conceivable situation. The information and metrics on how a team has done in the past are obviously valuable enough to merit the investment of a great deal of effort, time, and money.

Some business organizations measure the criteria and statistics related to a particular project in enough detail that evaluation can provide a wealth of valuable information about processes and performance and how to improve them. Some organizations tie performance data to reward and performance-management systems. When information is accurately collected and interpreted, it provides a competitive edge to the organization and helps team members grow, leverage strengths, and overcome weaknesses. However, evaluating the work of a group doesn't necessarily require complex procedures or a great deal of time to accomplish.

Without employing scientific data-gathering methods, a group can gain a great deal of useful knowledge by simply committing to, reflecting, learning, and reviewing each project as it concludes. This evaluation may take the form of a debriefing at a team meeting or a one-on-one discussion with individual team members.

The following questions help objectively assess what has been achieved and what has been learned from each task or project:

> "(about the past) . . . you can either run from it, or learn from it."
>
> *Anonymous*

1. Were the goals established at the beginning of the project achieved?

2. How well did we anticipate and work through obstacles?

3. Are similar obstacles likely to arise in the future? Is there something inherent in the organization's systems and culture that would get in the way of future tasks?

4. What else can we learn?

5. What can be done better next time?

6. What kind of preparation, planning, resources, or information is needed before beginning the project/task?

7. Do the systems, culture, and structure of the organization provide support to team members as they try new things?

8. Are people free to work together in creative, synergistic ways to achieve things that haven't been done before?

9. What factors prevent effectiveness and hinder success both individually and as a group?

10. Are team members held accountable for commitments?

Questions like these can provide the framework for discussion and exploration of important issues.

Whether evaluation and accountability are built into a formal performance management process, or team members simply make a personal commitment to learning from each completed project, the evaluation process can generate powerful opportunities for growth and change. It's been said that the definition of insanity is to "keep doing the same thing, while expecting different results." Consistent evaluation of performance identifies new or different things that need to be done to change the results.

Checklist for Facilitators

Facilitators should consider these key skills as they work to sustain the efforts of the group:

- ✦ Follow-up frequently on the action plan with team members (e-mail reminders, check-in, etc.)

- ✦ Create opportunities for the team member to be successful as they continue to act on plans or decisions.

- ✦ Encourage experimentation.

- ✦ Take a visible interest in team members' progress.

- ✦ Recognize and reward milestones.

- ✦ Be a coach.

- ✦ Demonstrate your focus and commitment.

- ✦ Solicit feedback on the communication process and procedures.

- ✦ Solicit facilitator feedback.

- ✦ Be responsive, and acknowledge complaints/concerns.

Tips for Team Members

One of the most commonly missed steps to getting things accomplished in teams, is to evaluate what has happened in the past. When you complete a project (or your part of the plan), you can learn a great deal about how to improve things in the future, by looking at how things went this time.

Follow Through on Commitments

✔ Make it a point to follow through on assignments, commitments, and tasks.

✔ Ask questions and clarify anything you're uncertain about.

Evaluate Your Performance

✔ Did you achieve what you set out to achieve?

✔ Were you able to deliver on your commitments within the time constraints?

Evaluate the Team's Success

✔ Did the team succeed in its goal?

✔ What obstacles did the team have to overcome along the way?

Evaluate Your Process

✔ How well did the team work together?

✔ Could the way the team interacted, communicated, and executed the plan be improved in any way?

✔ What did your team learn from this experience?

Part I

of *Leading Groups to Solutions* has introduced a model for facilitation that will guide you through a variety of situations.

Part II

narrows the focus to specific skills that you can use as you move through various steps of the Model. These "how-to's" will contribute to your effectiveness in any facilitation experience.

CHAPTER 10

Prepare to Facilitate

CHAPTER 10

Prepare to Facilitate

This book addresses specific measures that will lead to more effective facilitation. Regardless of the project or task, there is another level of preparation to consider: a person's readiness to act as a facilitator. A facilitator faces a myriad of situations, some of which test one's facilitation skills, patience, relationships, and character.

Although this book teaches practical principles for working with groups more effectively, facilitation isn't like a set of paint-by-number techniques. Likewise, it isn't about manipulating the group to come around to a certain point of view, although sometimes a facilitator may have to point out the benefits of a certain course of action and guide the group's direction within pre-defined parameters.

A facilitator frequently feels torn between the "task" — the objectives dictated by the organization, and the "relationship" — the bonds created among team members. A facilitator has to walk the tightrope between the needs and desires of team members and the expectations of other stakeholders outside the group.

The unique and challenging role of facilitator requires a significant level of preparation and the flexibility to change hats as the situation demands. An effective facilitator understands the challenge at hand, marshals the resources and talents of each team member, and organizes group efforts into a powerful force for change.

Character is an important quality in a facilitator. A facilitator needs to be the kind of person team members will follow into battle, someone they can trust and can rely upon when tough decisions need to be made. Team members inevitably question a facilitator's judgment, intentions, and conviction. Passing these tests creates a store of trust that helps both the facilitator and group through difficult times.

It is helpful to evaluate a person's readiness to facilitate, as well as the type of group. A person considering facilitation should ask the following questions:

+ How do I characterize the quality of my relationship with the group?

+ Do I enjoy a level of trust and alignment with team members?

+ Do team members look to me for leadership, answers, and the resources they need to succeed?

+ Do I need to mend some fences, build some bridges, and create a stronger connection between myself and some members of the team?

+ Are there gaps in my knowledge of the challenges the group faces?

+ Do I clearly understand what my team members face each day?

+ Am I in touch with the concerns, frustrations, and difficulties that team members face?

An honest assessment may reveal a high level of confidence, ability, and knowledge, as well as a healthy, positive relationship with other team members. However, the assessment may also identify gaps, areas requiring improvement, and the need for personal or relationship changes in which case additional preparation is necessary to ensure successful facilitation.

Tips for Team Members

Everyone eventually has the opportunity to lead a group. Personal and professional evaluation identifies the type of preparation required to become an effective leader.

Facilitator Types

✔ Whose leadership and group facilitation skills do you admire?

✔ What is your personal style? Are you able to connect easily and effectively with people?

✔ Are you the kind of person that others would follow if they didn't have to?

✔ Create a profile of leadership and facilitation skills that you want to develop or emulate.

Building Trust and Relationships Today

✔ How would you characterize your relationships with other team members?

✔ Do team members see you as someone personally reliable and worthy of their trust?

✔ What can you do to reach out to and connect with team members?

✔ Identify one or more team members (or leaders) with whom you will work to develop your relationship.

✔ Are you consistent in following through on the commitments you make?

CHAPTER 11

Create Great
Questions

CHAPTER 11

Create Great
Questions

Good questions stimulate interest and involvement, provide an opportunity for team members to use their talents, and are the core of successful communication in a group. Questions are an effective tool for facilitators because people enjoy being asked to respond. Questions are their ticket to participate and take ownership for the group's task. And questions serve an additional purpose of providing fresh insights, because facilitators don't always know the answers they'll get.

"You can tell whether a man is clever by his answers. You can tell whether a man is wise by his questions."

Naguib Mahfouz

When team members are asked for thoughts and ideas, facilitators give them an opportunity to participate in the problem-solving process. Questions put team members on their toes and establish an expectation of participation and contribution.

Questions help the facilitator accomplish a number of goals:

✦ Gather information

✦ Solve problems

✦ Focus thinking

✦ Set direction

✦ Build ownership

- ✦ Defuse conflict

- ✦ Open up dialogue

- ✦ Create and discover

- ✦ Confront tough issues

- ✦ Clarify understanding

Sometimes getting the best ideas and thinking from a group is as simple as just asking. It doesn't mean that everything the group comes up with will pan out, but most discussions reveal a few "nuggets" that are truly worthwhile. To get those really great ideas, you may need to sift through a lot of ore. You'll find that successful solutions and innovative ideas emerge from the group when the facilitator creates a climate of open communication.

How can a facilitator create the right platform for open dialogue?

Invite Gently

An invitation to participate should be easy and gentle, not abrupt.

- ✦ "Will you . . . "

- ✦ "Can you . . ."

- ✦ "Do you mind. . ."

Make a Request

Be specific and informative when assigning tasks and projects.

- ✦ Describe

- ✦ Explain

- ✦ Share

- ✦ Elaborate

- ✦ Show/Tell

+ Clarify

+ Talk

+ Enlighten

Guide & Target

Guide the respondents, and focus on the target of the question:

+ Thoughts

+ Experiences

+ Data

+ Knowledge

+ Skills

+ Reasoning

+ Logic

+ Perceptions

+ Senses

+ Intuition

+ Reactions

+ Insights

A good, open-ended question sounds like this:

> "A wise man's
> question contains
> half the answer."
> *Solomon ibn Gabirol*

+ "Can you share your experience with . . .?"

+ "Can you show us how you handled a difficult customer?"

+ "Can you describe your reasoning for this new plan?"

+ "Can you share your explanation of the data with us?"

All of these questions invite explanation and elaboration. When gently probing for additional information, use two or three follow-up questions. Asking and responding to effective, open-ended questions takes effort. Open-ended questions get people involved. Facilitators need to pay close attention and show respect for the response even when it's out in left field. Like all of the skills discussed in this book, good questioning techniques take practice, but can be developed.

There is no guarantee that every question will produce a "home run." When open-ended questions are overused or team members begin to feel manipulated, they'll quit responding genuinely. So it's important for the facilitator to stay connected to the discussion and shift the tone at appropriate intervals. When the time is right, don't be afraid to say, "Will everyone support this decision?" or "Can you do your part on the plan by mid-month?" or "Can you start the project now?"

When team members feel motivated, stimulated, and engaged by open-ended questions, the best ideas emerge. Good questions also help gain and measure team-member commitment to the plan, tasks, and projects.

Tips for Team Members

Great facilitators learn the art of asking questions to get every-one involved. Team members, too, can use questions to clarify and focus the group and to ensure that everyone is on the same page.

Ask Your Own Questions

✔ Do you jump in and ask questions when you don't understand?

✔ Are you embarrassed to ask questions, thinking it reveals that you don't already know something?

✔ Are you willing to ask questions if you think the group may be on the wrong track?

✔ Can you make a commitment to ask questions when you're unclear about what is going on?

Participate and Respond

✔ Do you support your leaders by actively responding to questions they raise?

✔ What can you do to become more knowledgeable and in-formed about the challenges your group is facing?

CHAPTER 12

Listen

Listen

One of the most discussed, but least practiced communication skills is effective listening. Whether leading or participating in a group, everybody has witnessed occasions where productivity suffers because group members are busily thinking about what they'll say next, rather than listening to what is being said by others. Listening is an underutilized facilitation technique that can enhance the team's productivity and clarity of purpose.

> "No one ever lost his job by listening too much."
>
> *Calvin Coolidge*

Exercising listening skills is extremely important during the "Clarify" phase of the facilitation process, but it is valuable at other key intervals in the process as well. In fact, when group members fail to listen, the facilitation can grind to a halt, regardless of the phase, because failing to listen results in a failure to communicate. It's been said that "We all have two ears, and one mouth, and we ought to use them proportionately."

Listening allows a facilitator to capture and verify information from individual team members, and to re-state, summarize, and communicate it to the group as a whole. If done well, listening not only contributes to the level of trust and support within a team, but also encourages team members to contribute ideas, feelings, and perspectives. Active listening allows deeper meanings and issues to surface.

Listening is not a passive activity; it requires commitment and attention. Most people listen in "spurts," tuning in and out, cued occasionally by words or silences that capture attention, wondering what was missed. Listening experts believe that people remember only half of what was heard, and that within 48 hours, the retention of new information drops to approximately 7%. Some of this loss is inevitable, but active listening allows people to categorize and connect important points.

Information often is disorganized and difficult to understand. In a group setting, amid lively discussion and debate, it is challenging to sift through and capture the relevant points. As a facilitator, there is value in establishing ground rules for speaking and listening, so that each team member can be heard and the best ideas can be captured.

Everyone can improve personal listening skills. However, in a group, listening is important primarily because of the need to monitor and manage the flow of information. Listening to team members is critical because it conveys a sense of how much they are valued. Listening halfheartedly or becoming distracted by other information sends a message to the speaker that something else is more important at that moment. Don't kid yourself — people know when they are being listened to.

> "The most important thing in communication is to hear what isn't being said."
>
> *Peter F. Drucker*

Regardless of the setting, practice can improve listening skills. People can learn to concentrate and focus on the "heart of the message." Key points may not be found in words but in tone, manner, and attitude. Listening with more than your ears draws out important information never recognized in the words alone.

There are three keys to effective listening in a group setting:

1. Withhold Judgment

Remain objective and avoid assumptions. Recognize when you are judging others or what they are saying. Clear your mind of biases and opinions, and focus on complete neutrality. Withholding judgment and criticism draws out deeper meanings and builds a foundation of trust.

Facial expressions and body language also reveals feelings. Hearing things that you disagree with, you may be tempted to rebut them immediately. Instead, try to understand the speaker's perspective.

People sometimes jump to conclusions based on the language of the message. Certain words and phrases trigger emotions, and people hear what they want to hear. It's important to break down assumptions by focusing on what is actually said. Avoiding assumptions and really listening result in understanding team or group members in ways you may never have before.

There are other barriers to effective listening, for example, paying attention only to those parts of the message that are interesting. People may also "tune out" things deemed irrelevant. Sometimes even the personal charisma or entertainment value of a speaker can increase or decrease the level at which people focus on the message.

2. Stay Tuned to the Impact of Personal Filters

Everyone has learned to interpret the world uniquely, based on such filters as personal past experiences, memories, beliefs, emotions,  attitudes, interests, or values. There is an old story of a group of blind men who happen upon an elephant and are asked to describe it. The man holding the trunk observes that an elephant must be like a snake, the man touching the tusks concludes that an elephant must be like a spear, and so on. For each man, reality is based on his limited perceptions. So personal filters limit a person's ability to truly listen and understand.

Filters can cause listening skills to break down, because people jump to conclusions with just a little bit of information. When discussing something people have strong opinions about, their emotional filters can cloud judgment and perception. Rather than listening for understanding, people tune out the speaker and plan a response in order to "stay ahead" in the debate.

Every team member has filters. They, too, jump to conclusions, rush to judgment, and assume that they understand. A facilitator can do much to limit the negative impact of filters by setting an example of open, accepting listening and by conveying the message that everyone can be heard and understood.

3. Check for Understanding

Last, and probably most important, summarize and check for understanding. Summarizing verifies how accurately the message was heard. Summarizing also clarifies the message for other team members who may not have listened to or understood what was communicated. The following statements or questions can be used to check understanding:

> "Never assume, seldom deny, always distinguish."
>
> *Anonymous*

✦ "What I heard you say is . . ."

✦ "John, do you feel I have accurately summarized your perspective?"

✦ "Pat, were you referring to the cost control program?"

Listen for jargon, slang, acronyms, and other key terms that all team members might not understand. For example, "Does everyone understand what Karen means when she says 'lean thinking'?"

This quick check helps ascertain the quality of the information collected. Ask yourself; "Do I know the what, when, where, how, who, and why?" Don't be afraid to tell the speaker that you don't understand, with language like this:

✦ "I am not clear what you mean."

✦ "How does that tie into this situation?"

✦ "Can you explain that in greater detail?"

Becoming aware of personal filters and tendencies improves the quality and depth of listening skills. Conveying interest in team members enables them to openly share what's on their mind. The group enjoys higher trust, more open communication, and greater contribution by each team member to a shared direction, purpose, and tasks when a culture of listening is developed.

Tips for Team Members

Learning to listen well is one of life's greatest skills, both in professional and personal endeavors. Poor listening is one of the greatest obstacles to working effectively toward group solutions. How do you rate when it comes to listening?

Are You Listening?

✔ Do you come to team meetings and discussions ready to participate?

✔ Do you sit in the back and catch up on your work, stay under the radar, and keep a low profile?

✔ When you participate, are you trying to understand why certain questions are asked or topics are raised?

Are Your Filters On?

✔ Do you have an attitude of, "I've heard this before," that might get in the way of effective listening?

✔ Are you open to new ideas and possibilities, and interested in becoming part of the solution?

✔ Do you screen out some people in your group (including the facilitator) because you don't think they have much to offer?

CHAPTER 13

Anchor Your Team

Anchor Your Team

Whenever a team comes together to address a situation, it is important to define a purpose or problem statement. This process is called "dropping the anchor." It may be a long-standing team or an ad hoc committee; the issues may be "normal" business challenges or a special project; the setting may be a weekly staff meeting or a luncheon discussion about a new project. Regardless of the situation, defining a purpose or problem statement early on anchors the team and keeps it from drifting in the turbulent water of open discussion.

Defining a purpose or problem statement doesn't always need to be a formal or complicated process. Sometimes, it's just a discussion to ensure that the group's goals and purposes are clear and accepted by everyone. More complex projects may require a document that outlines the goals, objectives, and parameters the group needs to follow in defining and implementing a solution.

The purpose or problem statement should specifically define the product, deliverable, or outcome that represents success for the group. A skilled facilitator asks a few simple questions that help the team gain clarity about the problem or decision, and also reveal any tangential problems or decisions. Deeper issues that surface may need to be dissected into more manageable segments.

A facilitator generally has a clear idea of the challenge or problem prior to the group discussion. Why not spell out the agenda rather than take the time to clarify why the team has come together? Open discussion reveals what team members do and don't know, and it identifies other topics that the facilitator may not have initially recognized. Different priorities and viewpoints will also emerge, and the facilitator can gain a better perspective on the situation. Further, an open discussion provides team members with an excellent opportunity to get engaged in the problem, feel ownership for the task, and begin thinking about how they can contribute.

The good news is that defining the purpose or problem statement can be a very simple process. Questions like the following will help frame the objective:

✦ "How do you define the task or problem?"

✦ "What are the key issues that need to be addressed today?"

✦ "What needs to be decided?"

✦ "What is the number one priority of the group today?"

Open-ended questions like these direct and focus the discussion. Let the questions do the work. The answer to one question may stimulate another question that helps the group more clearly define the objectives. As a facilitator, give ample opportunity for everyone to contribute; then distill the information into major points or themes. These points should be measurable or quantitative/qualitative indicators of success.

The purpose or problem statement should not include the solution or the root causes of the situation. The goal here is to clarify what needs to be done, addressed, or fixed. The purpose or problem statement is an anchoring point, helping the team maintain its bearings as it proceeds. As the group moves from defining the problem to analyzing and diagnosing the solution, it may encounter obstacles, distractions, and side issues that could lead away from the central task. By calling the group's attention to a well-defined purpose or problem statement, a facilitator can help the group stay on task, while creating action plans that meet the group's objectives.

Tips for Team Members

The weekly meetings of long-standing teams can seem like meaningless repetition, a rehashing of the same issues and concerns. Even groups formed to solve a specific problem can sometimes suffer from a lack of focus or too broad a scope. How well do you know what your team is supposed to accomplish?

What is Your Team's Purpose?

✔ Are you clear about your team's goals, purpose, and assignments?

✔ Can you see how your team's objectives tie into those of the larger group, division, or organization?

✔ Do you see misalignment or misunderstanding among team members as to your purpose?

Buying In to the Vision

✔ How do you feel about your role in your group?

✔ Do you believe in and feel committed to the vision?

✔ Are there areas of your team's purpose in which you feel no passion or agreement?

Resolving Disconnects

✔ How can you connect what you feel passionately about to the purpose of your team?

✔ Can you consider discussing your feelings with your leader, adjusting your views, or moving to another group?

✔ Can you take some time to identify how to more fully align your goals and objectives with those of your team?

CHAPTER 14

Establish Ground Rules: Don't Build Your House on the Sand

Establish Ground Rules: Don't Build Your House on the Sand

We recently found ourselves in a situation that may be familiar to several organizations. We have a weekly staff meeting over lunch every Friday. On this particular week, the meeting was scheduled for 11:30, and one of the team members was assigned to order and pick up lunch. When I arrived at the conference room at 11:30, I found the following circumstances:

1. Only 3 of 19 team members were present.

2. One of these three team members announced that he had to run home to return his car to his wife.

3. One team member was on a conference call.

4. The team member in charge of lunch forgot to pre-order the food and didn't leave the office until 11:25 to pick it up.

5. As for everyone else — your guess is as good as mine!

By 12:00, the entire team finally gathered in the conference room, drawn more by the smell of the late-arriving food than anything else. Thirty minutes late, the meeting finally started.

How many times has your team been in a similar situation? How many meetings have begun, or failed to begin, like this? How often do team members arrive late to meetings, bringing various agendas and still caught up in the last task? Some team members bring other work to meetings, hoping to stay quiet and get some "real work" done while pretending to listen.

The situation with our Friday staff meeting was upsetting. However, even more upsetting was the realization that these practices and attitudes had grown when it should have been addressed sooner. It's obvious that some counterproductive norms had been created. Ironically, team leaders only contribute to the problem by not emphasizing expectations, especially with new team members. Leaders are occasionally late, preoccupied, or involved in other things as well, which is sure to convey a confusing message to other team members.

This may seem like a minor issue, but it's certainly common in many organizations. As a result of the Friday meeting occurrence, we did a few calculations. By arriving late or not attending this team meeting, time had been wasted at the rate of a half an hour per person on the team. Multiplied by 19 team members, a total of 9-1/2 hours had been wasted. Multiplied by 52 weeks in a year, up to 494 hours could be wasted, totaling a loss of several thousands of dollars in a year's time. It's astonishing how one simple habit can affect the bottom line.

> One of the keys to working together effectively is to ensure that each team member understands the ground rules or norms for that team.

In fact, most team activities are simple: meetings, discussions, tasks, and projects. Team members interact with each other in fairly predictable, repetitive ways. One of the keys to working together effectively is to ensure that each team member understands the ground rules or norms for that team.

Ground rules are the guiding principles that define what is and is not acceptable behavior in a group. Ground rules express what both facilitators and team members need to do, and how objectives are to be accomplished in order to make the time spent together efficient and successful. Ground rules include information on group behavior, how meetings work, and the interaction process between team members. Establishing ground rules usually prevents misunderstandings and disagreements. Ground rules also establish a team climate and culture that are conducive to creative thinking and problem solving.

Ground rules don't need to be overly complex or exhaustive. They simply need to create a productive foundation for group discussions. Ground rules can be stated, documented, even unspoken. However, establishing ground rules with the input of the group not only prevents future frustration, but also creates greater buy-in, commitment, and support. When negotiating ground rules, team members create a "contract," which is simply an agreement. Successful agreements have two parts: mutual consent (people choose to participate) and valid consideration (everyone benefits from cooperation). If these two conditions are met, ground rules should be negotiated.

There's an old parable about a wise man and a foolish man. The wise man built his house on a rock foundation, while the foolish man built his house on the sand. Failing to establish ground rules is like building a house on sand. While it may seem okay initially, the foundation is unstable and will crumble when the first storm blows through. Every team experiences some foul weather, including pressure, adversity, and  dissension. When a team establishes and commits to live by a set of storm-proof ground rules, the team builds on a rock foundation. These teams are able to withstand stormy discussions, difficult topics, and challenging projects.

Our team had a habit of lax attendance and promptness to team meetings, just one simple indicator that forecasted an emerging problem and the need for clearer ground rules. Ground rules say a lot about respect, the esteem in which team members hold each other, and the value team members place upon the collective time and efforts of the group. Consider some of the following "rocks" or areas in which developing solid ground rules establishes a strong base for group decision-making.

1. Create a Safe Place

How "safe" is your current team environment? Is there a high degree of trust among team members? Do team members feel comfortable sharing ideas and opinions? Can team members address differences of opinion, confront difficult issues, and challenge unacceptable situations or behavior without aggressively attacking other members?

Ground rules can address appropriate language, respect for each opinion, and valuing diverse viewpoints and backgrounds. They may also address a willingness to be open and vulnerable, not taking yourselves too seriously, supporting one another, and persisting in open, honest dialogue until solutions are found and problems are solved.

2. Have Each Team Member Contribute

Each team member should understand and feel personally responsible to contribute to the success of the group. This might include timeliness, follow through, reliability, and being fully present while participating in group discussion.

3. Establish Ground Rules for Decision Making/Gaining Consensus

What is your team's decision-making style? How do you come to an agreement, especially when team members hold widely different views? When decisions are reached, by what process do you gain true consensus and ownership? How do you help each team member find ways to honestly support the plan?

Ground rules can be established for the brainstorming process to ensure that all ideas are heard and that it doesn't turn into "blame" storming. Ground rules define a "tiebreaker" or identify a "veto power" process. Previously established processes help when the group reaches an impasse or becomes deadlocked on an issue.

4. Create Accountability for Tasks and Projects

Some teams do a great job of planning and problem-solving, only to lose focus and commitment after the meeting is over. Ground rules can be established around record keeping, accountability for task and project commitments, and timelines for completion. These initial rules can extend beyond the ground discussion. Teams can define and commit to a process of making commitments and assignments, as well as maintaining a focus on these commitments until they are completed.

Ground rules established by the team, have the greatest impact over time. An effective facilitator draws out ideas, provides suggestions, and subtly directs the conversation, but group participation is key.

Open-ended questions serve as a valuable tool for provoking team members to share ground-rule ideas. Consider the following:

+ What are attendance expectations?

+ What are participation expectations?

+ What communication skills will support the group's efforts?

+ What does consensus mean?

+ What is collectively important to the group?

+ What does the group value?

When facilitating a group that has never operated with ground rules, prepare for the session by creating a list of some ideas and suggestions that will spur the team's thought processes. Team members can also come prepared with their own ideas. Initially, brainstorm a starter list with the group. Be sure that the list is simple and straightforward, 10-12 items or less. The list of ground rules can always be added to, or subtracted from. New situations or dynamics may require new guidelines, so make the ground rules a flexible living contract that can be re-negotiated. Revisit and revise the ground rules as needs and expectations change.

Whenever possible, display the team's ground rules to ensure that they stay fresh on everyone's mind. It may be helpful to post the ground rules in the meeting or conference room. A visual of the ground rules can also be an anchor and reminder for team members if reinforcement is necessary. Capture the essence of the ground rules in short, action-oriented statements. Consider the following sample:

+ Listen.

+ Make no personal attacks; use "I" statements.

+ Value diversity, creativity, and differences of opinion.

+ Arrive on time.

+ Avoid side conversations.

+ Support team decisions outside of the meeting.

+ Recognize that silence is not consensus.

Early on, it may be helpful to evaluate or even "score" how well the group is following the original ground rules. An assessment provides an indicator for adjustments or clarification.

In some situations, although ground rules are established, different group norms evolve. For example, a ground rule is set that team meetings start at 11:30. However, a norm may develop where people don't arrive until exactly 11:30. Therefore, the meeting doesn't begin until 11:35. In this situation, the facilitator needs to decide how precisely to enforce the ground rule. Some ground rules are firm, if not absolute, and these should be carefully monitored. Other ground rules are flexible, subject to adjustment or redefinition according to what the group is willing to support. However, ground rules that aren't respected and enforced rapidly lose power and credibility.

> . . . ground rules that aren't respected and enforced rapidly lose power and credibility.

Some ground rules represent the ideal situation. For example, a ground rule may be established that requires everyone to openly share his/her suggestions and opinions. However, if the prevailing culture is one where people are punished for being open and honest, or if team members become defensive when their behavior is questioned, it is difficult to encourage team members to support this ground rule. If the team is to develop an environment where ideas can grow and flourish, facilitators need to demonstrate enough courage to discuss and confront gaps with the group.

Establishing ground rules helps team members perform at a highly productive level and in a manner that helps each team member grow, develop, and increase his/her willingness and ability to contribute.

Looking back at our situation, we have invested a few extra minutes to establish some clear ground rules, enabling the team to accomplish more and stay on task. A simple discussion about group expectations has paved the way to a more healthy and productive team culture.

Every team develops its own well-defined, accepted, and formal or informal rules for operation. The most effective groups, however, consciously determine how to operate.

Tips for Team Members

Every team develops over time its own rules for operation, whether they be formal or informal, well-defined or simply accepted as norms. The most effective groups, however, consciously determine how they'll operate, from how they treat each other and communicate together, to how they resolve differences when they arise.

Do Team Members Know the Rules?

✔ Does the group have formalized ground rules for communication, resolving differences, and planning?

✔ Does the group need better defined rules to be more effective?

✔ Is the group environment more formal or informal?

Contributing to the Creation of Ground Rules

✔ What suggestions can each team member make for rules for the group?

✔ What would make the group more effective?

✔ Do unhealthy or dysfunctional patterns of communication, leadership, or discussion exist within the group?

CHAPTER 15

Get Comfortable
with Tension

Get Comfortable with Tension

What is Tension?

O ver time, groups that effectively interact discover an essential truth: a little tension is critical to success. Stress is essential for growth, not a negative, destructive stress, but a positive, "testing of the system" type of stress. Just as muscles need to be stretched and exposed to tension in order to grow, so too with teams and groups: they increase their capacity through facing challenging experiences.

It's important to strike a balance. In the hu-  man body, for example, there is a normal, healthy range for blood pressure. Too much, and you run the risk of blowing out a blood vessel, or worse, the system entirely shuts down. Too little, and the heart can't deliver the blood that makes the system thrive. An effective facilitator finds the right time to put some pressure on the group, and knows when to back off and cut the group some slack.

Some people, however, shy away from tension and conflict in the workplace. People have been conditioned to think that everyone should be polite, politically correct, and non-confrontational — the classic definition of cooperation. In many work environments, team members have learned that saying what's on their mind has negative repercussions. Disagreement is viewed as being uncooperative, disloyal, or "not a team player."

Developing a comfort level with healthy tension, open discussion, and active debate does not mean becoming abrasive, attacking, or rude. When team members feel free and safe to really express opinions, great ideas surface and flourish.

The key to this healthy, messy, and noisy process is the facilitator. The facilitator helps the group strike a balance between constructive tension and supportiveness, consideration, emotional safety, and comfort. High-performing teams eliminate the fear of retribution by creating a safe place where difficult and sensitive issues can be discussed. In fact, effective groups recognize the need to raise sensitive issues.

> When team members feel free and safe to really express opinions, great ideas surface and flourish.

The facilitator creates safety by establishing well-defined ground rules and norms that promote open disclosure and insist that team members don't address differences in a personal way. Although ground rules were discussed in a separate chapter, a group culture that promotes tolerance and understanding between team members is essential to this process. The free flow of information, ideas, and constructive critique has to be encouraged. A facilitator generally has to ask for these behaviors. Most team members aren't inclined to offer this kind of input or feedback voluntarily. On the other hand, some team members may be overly willing, harsh, or abrupt. The facilitator also has to be willing to take risks and be open, both in stating opinions and in receiving ideas from team members.

Some groups are afraid that open argument will raise unhealthy emotions and breed ill will. Open discussion is not the same as aggression, destruction, and disorder. Frank and candid debate, focusing on the issues, creates new opportunities, generates fresh ideas, and instills energy and excitement in the team. Conflict and the airing of differences provide fuel for creativity, which results from exploring alternative views, raising challenges, and hearing different perspectives.

Promoting a healthy dose of diversity is essential to getting the group out of its comfort level and avoiding a "fixed mental set." Groups often respond to new problems by employing the same approach that was used to solve previous, similar issues. Effective groups require people to be on different mental tracks, with divergent views and ideas. It has been said if two people in a discussion feel exactly the same way, then one of them is unnecessary.

Some factors and conditions can limit open discussion and lead to people feeling censored in what they say:

+ Strong personalities

+ Overuse of authority

+ Fear of personal attacks

+ Doubts and lack of commitment to the task

+ Fear of ostracism from the group

+ Time constraints

+ Fear of challenging the status quo

The "Abilene Paradox"

Jerry Harvey introduced one of the more notable examples of unhealthy group communication dynamics in what he calls the "Abilene Paradox." Harvey contends that many groups are so concerned with avoiding conflict that they end up in an insidious cycle of collusion. That is, they appear to be in cooperation and agreement because no one expresses dissatisfaction and lack of consensus. Under the thin veil of surface harmony is a boiling pot of negative emotion and unexpressed issues. People publicly agree because it is the safe way to operate, allowing unresolved problems to ferment out of sight. When team members are unwilling to honestly speak up, the group may, ironically, adopt ideas and take actions contrary to its own wishes and needs. Groups suffering from the "Abilene Paradox" may default to what they think their leaders want, or worse, what seems to be the least threatening course of action. Above all else, team members must be willing to test the open water and boldly make contributions. People can't sit back and wait for the right time to weigh in. Aubrey Fisher suggests that the sooner people "enter the fray," the better. If input comes too late in the process, it actually gets in the way of group progress.

The willingness to challenge and dissent is only likely to occur in an environment where the facilitator sets the appropriate tone, establishes safety, and encourages and rewards participation. Facilitators have to support spontaneity and candor, rather than worry excessively as to how input will be perceived. Each team member must feel a responsibility and the freedom to contribute ideas and make suggestions.

> The willingness to challenge and dissent is only likely to occur in an environment where the facilitator sets the appropriate tone, establishes safety, and encourages and rewards participation.

In some cultures, tension and confrontation are seen as taboo. In these situations, people are very uncomfortable with challenging ideas, speaking their mind, and openly addressing sensitive subjects. In many groups, team members respectfully defer to authority figures and fail to register their concerns, thoughts, and contributions.

It requires some sensitivity to be able to state opinions without causing defensiveness in others. Someone will likely feel responsible when another team members points out an undesirable situation or contrary view. Feeling put on the spot, team members may respond with defensiveness. The key is to reduce emotional content by being honest, matter-of-fact, and by expressing concerns provisionally as something to consider, rather than with certainty.

Certainty

Some team members may be perfectly comfortable being open and direct. In fact, they may engage in overly confrontational behavior in the name of honesty and openness. One attitude that can cause a stumbling block to open communication is "certainty." Certainty means that a team member is absolutely sure that there is only one way to look at a particular situation (black or white, right or wrong), or only one solution to the problem.

People like this present positions as absolute fact, thereby closing the door to open discussion. When a facilitator or team member presents a position with absolute certainty, it takes an equally strong personality to push back on that position. On the other hand, when a position is presented provisionally, simply as "one idea worth thinking about," others feel free to respond, present alternatives, and even point out strengths and weaknesses.

Facilitators can generally learn to be more open-minded, flexible, and provisional. Group discussions aren't an argument to be won or grounds to be conquered and claimed. Let the most effective ideas win. It is not an issue of *who* is right, but *what* is right.

> **It is not an issue of *who* is right, but *what* is right.**

When presenting ideas, begin with a caveat or a disclaimer. One approach is, "I know what our customers want and how they'll react to this idea." Another approach is, "I've talked to three of our customers, and they seem to feel that our initial proposal to implement. This is a small sample, of course, so I'm interested in getting a few more viewpoints."

What Is Normal?

In the end, groups that avoid tension and conflict miss out on great discoveries. Groups appearing to be in harmony may struggle with implementation of ideas because they really haven't reached a consensus or tapped into the creative forces of the group.

Excessive tension, too, can be harmful, as it can result in different points of view not getting presented or responded to with respect and consideration. Healthy tension and emotion imply activity and investment by team members vs. apathy and disinterest.

Problems inevitably arise in any group. There are differences of opinion (hidden or exposed), strongly held beliefs, personal biases, and blind spots. A group is not going to agree all the time on the best way to solve a problem. The facilitator's responsibility is to keep the tension at a healthy level, explore differences, and encourage expression.

Adversity and controversy are normal, and groups need to get used to them and learn to work through them. Too many groups avoid tension, hoping that it will go away, rather than learning to deal with it and manage it. Don't be afraid of focused, active. Groups that are engaged in this type of discussion, are not headed down the road to "Abilene." When team members defend positions without attacking and respond to discussion without defensiveness, groups engage in behavior that strengthens the group. When team members disagree without being disagreeable, they are learning to work through tension in healthy ways.

The Facilitator's Role

As a facilitator, if apparent harmony in the group appears suspicious, stop and check for discontent. Ask the group, challenge team members, and point out that little discord or contrary views are being expressed. It may be that the group has reached consensus, or it may be that issues are being avoided that ought to be discussed.

Effective groups are aggressive, loud at times, and willing to have "gutsy" dialogue. Don't bottle up constructive tension, but don't let it boil over into negative feelings, personal attacks, or personal agendas either.

The following guidelines can help a facilitator keep the tension level balanced:

1. Decide to honestly confront issues head-on (don't avoid or ignore).

2. Define ground rules and guidelines at the onset to maintain open debate.

3. Keep a "finger on the pulse;" monitor when the tension level is too high or too low.

4. Be willing to "name it." State what you see or feel. Test observations out with the group, and make the group "own the problem" if the tension is to high.

5. Be willing to play the "devil's advocate;" advocate worthwhile, opposing positions to test the strength of the group's consensus.

6. Mediate when conflict escalates or becomes personal.

7. Relieve tension by stepping back, laughing, and relaxing a little.

8. Let the group occasionally vent frustrations around events outside of their control. Be careful not to abdicate responsibility for solutions. Complain a little about "outside forces" if necessary, but don't create too many enemies or scapegoats, or turn the discussion into a "gripe session."

9. Let the tension lead to new possibilities and creative options. Tension keeps team members searching and thinking about different solutions.

10. Don't let debates and arguments delay healthy group discussion and create defensiveness. Stay open, and clarify the motives and intentions of others in a one-on-one discussion to clear up any misunderstandings.

11. Be patient, and give the group time to think, process, and reflect.

Testing, criticism, and scrutiny are normal and necessary to reach high-quality solutions. Team members must be willing to accept some rejection. Rejection of ideas doesn't mean rejection of self or of one's value to the group. Encourage team members not to take criticism personally, and not to offer it in a personal way.

Promote active verbal participation, ask thought-provoking questions, and be willing to dissent objectively. Promote creative abrasion. Tension stimulates critical-thinking faculties. Without conflict, "group think" occurs; people pull in, play it safe, and don't challenge the status quo.

The challenge with group tension and emotional discussion is not that it exists, but rather to create the right balance. With practice, groups learn to tolerate a healthy level of tension and grow through the experience. Constructively dealing with differences leads to consensus, ownership, high involvement, and concentrated effort; it promotes the search for new alternatives. A pattern of successful debate and tension helps build group cohesiveness and provides an outlet for frustration. Anything that enhances vibrant communication and healthy debate has to be looked upon as a positive force, one that leads the group to growth and maturity.

Tips for Team Members

Each group (and its individual members) has its own ways of dealing with conflict and tension. Some avoid it, tabling any discussion that threatens to get tense. Some groups seem to enjoy getting confrontational, playing out win-lose scenarios and trying to get the upper hand. But conflict is a fact of life, and we need to develop strategies for turning it into an opportunity to develop and surface new ideas and solutions.

What's Your Tolerance for Tension?

✔ What is your response to tension and conflict? Do you "fight" or "flee"?

✔ What's the environment on your team? Combative? Avoiding?

✔ What can you and your team do to improve your ability to deal with difficult topics?

Disagreeing Without Being Disagreeable

✔ Can you disagree with someone without getting too emotional or personal?

✔ What can you do to increase your understanding and tolerance for people you disagree with, or who irritate you?

Building Relationships in the Midst of Conflict

✔ Commit to spending some time talking to someone with whom you've had disagreements or conflicts.

✔ Commit to speak with respect, even when your views are different from someone else's.

✔ Be more provisional, less certain; listen to and ask for more information on opposing views.

CHAPTER 16

Deal with Defensiveness

Deal with Defensiveness

In a perfect world, facilitators would only work with high-energy, committed teams in an environment of openness and trust. Each team discussion would be conducted efficiently, and facilitators would enjoy the synergy of working with a unified group of people, willing to commit their best to each task.

However, in reality, every team has personalities, problems, histories, and issues. Some of these are long-standing groups that have a lot of experience and plenty of war stories. Some are newly formed teams, seeking to find purpose and identity, to define the ways in which they interact. Other groups are dysfunctional, with a history of distrust, difficulty, high emotions, and competitiveness.

Even in successful, high-performing groups, there are team members who lack trust or confidence and who express themselves defensively manner. Defensiveness is a significant obstacle to team unity and focus: at best, it creates distraction, and at worst, it is a cancer that eats at the foundations of your team.

When a team member manifests defensive behavior, the facilitator may automatically assume that the behavior is an intentional attempt to disrupt the group. It's important, however, to look closely at the causes of the behavior. Defensiveness may come from team members who lack confidence, feel attacked or disregarded, or may be feeling exposed and vulnerable.

Defensiveness may arise when team members feel as though they have been held up to ridicule or made the butt of inappropriate humor, whether by the team facilitator or by other team members. When the prevailing culture of a group is one of blame and personal criticism, stronger members protect themselves by going on the offensive, and weaker members may fall victim to the cycle of accusations and blame.

Defensiveness is all about threat. When team members feel threatened, or anticipate a threat, many go into a defensive mode, deflecting attention away from their shortcomings or retaliating for perceived unfairness. They lose focus on the task at hand and, in fact, may distract other team members from it as well. Rather than attending to the solution, team members spend energy and time evaluating how to defend themselves, thinking about how others see the situation, strategizing how to be seen more favorably, or analyzing how to win, dominate, or escape punishment.

A defensive outlook by just one or two team members can seriously limit the productivity of the entire group. In an attempt to shift blame, team members may point fingers at others, creating a vicious cycle that compromises the group's ability to achieve substantial results.

Creating a non-defensive group attitude necessitates accountability. Accountability requires team members to take responsibility for problems and commit to work together toward solutions. Defensive behavior indicates that team members are more worried about how they are seen than about solving the problems.

While it's generally *not* the facilitator's fault when team members express defensiveness, the facilitator can respond in ways that have a great deal to do with correcting the situation:

✦ Raise difficult topics, challenges, and problems without necessarily blaming someone.

✦ Focus on unacceptable situations or behaviors without being overly critical of the person.

+ Adjust his/her personal coaching style so as not to come across as too personal, critical, or subjective.

+ Choose the right wording and speech that allow the group to discover and problem-solve without pointing fingers.

Jack R. Gibb, Ph.D., a noted researcher and consultant, stated in *The Journal of Communication,* that facilitators can strongly impact the level of defensiveness in group interactions by the style in which they communicate. In the table below, Dr. Gibb identifies the characteristic facilitator behaviors that create either defensiveness or support.

SUPPORTIVE BEHAVIORS	DEFENSIVE BEHAVIORS
Description	Evaluation
Problem Orientation	Control
Spontaneity	Strategy
Empathy	Neutrality
Equality	Superiority
Provisional	Certainty

The behaviors outlined above represent choices by the facilitator: choices to speak and act in specific, intentional ways that reduce threat while focusing on the task. It is easy for team members (especially if they feel inadequate, guilty, or threatened) to perceive speech as judgmental, regardless of the intention. Therefore, the facilitator must think about ways to frame what is said in a style that conveys support.

Describe vs. Evaluate

Focus on statements and questions that refer to the task at hand, rather than those that convey judgment about how the team member is addressing the task:

+ "Based on your experience, how would you describe this situation?"

+ "What should we be paying attention to here?"

+ "It sounds like our biggest challenge is..."

+ "What areas do you think we need to focus on?"

Problem Orientation vs. Control

Problem orientation means that the facilitator conveys a willingness and desire to collaborate in defining the problem, seeking a solution, and avoiding personal agendas or preconceived notions about controlling the conclusion. Modern culture is so bombarded by media messages, trying to persuade people what to buy, how to think, and who to vote for, that people automatically suspect and resent messages that perceive to be controlling.

Here are some ideas for conveying problem orientation:

+ "I'd like to get your ideas on this..."

+ "How do you see this problem?"

+ "What do you think is the root cause?"

+ "I value your opinion on this and think you're closer to the situation than I am."

Spontaneity vs. Strategy

Be open and genuine. Don't withhold information, drop names, or hoard information. Team members are likely to feel resentment and become defensive when facilitators convey a know-it-all attitude.

Team members also respond negatively when they think that the facilitator is trying to manipulate them. Be relaxed, be authentic, and respond with sincerity. Use intuition, and share hunches and ideas freely. A facilitator should censor personal opinions, letting team members express ideas first. Team members are more inclined to open up if the facilitator models spontaneity.

Empathy vs. Neutrality

Demonstrate real concern for team members, and express appreciation for their value and contribution to the group. Facilitators who are unable to show respect, warmth, and caring rarely create solid connections with team members and are unable to build trust and create loyalty. Communication that conveys empathy for the feelings of team members reduces their tendency to feel defensive. It is reassuring when the facilitator expresses a true understanding of team members' concerns, obstacles, pressures, and challenges. Empathy means more than simply being neutral. Neutral means unbiased, which is important. But empathy means really knowing individual team members and understanding their goals and concerns.

Equality vs. Superiority

Whenever facilitators communicate a sense that they are superior in position, power, salary, intellectual ability, or experience, team members feel inadequate; become jealous, competitive, or defensive; or simply disengage from the discussion.

Regardless of position, a facilitator who conveys a sense of partnership builds alliances and sends a message of trust and respect. By emphasizing common purpose, the facilitator can rally the group around the task and they can operate as a team.

Provisionality vs. Certainty

The message of teamwork and unity is reinforced by letting answers come from within the group. A position stated with certainty, especially early in a discussion, can have a chilling effect on the participation, contribution, and willingness of group members to challenge ideas. Although a facilitator may already know the answer, communicating that fact too aggressively raises defensiveness.

Be willing to be flexible as new information emerges from group discussion. State ideas as options, not absolutes.

Avoid making statements like these:

✦ "There is only one way to do this."

✦ "I know for sure…"

✦ "There is no room for debate."

Defensiveness is inevitable and will emerge occasionally. It may be rooted in the culture of the team or be a temporary response from one particular team member. In any case, understanding reasons behind the behavior and the facilitator's options in addressing and reducing the defensiveness will help the group achieve its goals more effectively.

"To improve is to change; to be perfect is to change often."

Winston Churchill

Tips for Team Members

Defensiveness can be a significant obstacle to the effective work of teams. Defensive feelings may come in response to feeling as though we're being blamed or attacked when things go wrong. Sometimes we feel guilty because we realize we have fallen short in some way. Mostly, defensiveness arises in an environment of low trust, where people are more concerned about protecting themselves than about the task at hand.

Overcoming Defensive Feelings

✔ Do team members or leaders frequently get defensive in your group discussions?

✔ Are you inclined to feel or express defensiveness when things don't go well?

✔ Can you pause before responding to what seems like an attack? Focus on tasks and legitimate obstacles to performance, not on defending yourself.

✔ Are there areas in which you need to improve your performance or clarify expectations?

Defensiveness in Others

✔ Try to defuse defensiveness in others by focusing on tasks.

✔ Ask questions to gain greater understanding of what's not working.

✔ Offer appropriate assistance — be part of the solution.

Think
Creatively

Think Creatively

One of the greatest challenges for many teams is to get "out of the box" and come up with creative, new solutions. Groups tend to get locked into repetitive ways of interacting, thinking, and planning, which impede their ability to respond to new situations. Too often team members become comfortable with familiar and predictable methods, when what has worked in the past may not be sufficient to deal with emerging challenges.

Some teams and groups have a natural tendency toward creative thought; a few groups may even need to be reined in from time to time to maintain a practical perspective on problem-solving. However, it's a far more common situation for teams to get stuck on a problem, unable to come up with a novel or innovative solution.

A few simple steps to brainstorming and creative thinking will help teams when they are stuck. Whether the team is naturally creative or more cautious, these simple behaviors help groups to develop more powerful solutions.

The Creative Fuel

✦ Express the belief that there are no bad ideas.

✦ Be spontaneous and list ideas quickly

✦ Capture every initial suggestion; "quantity of ideas" is strongly desired.

✦ Encourage and acknowledge unique ideas.

✦ List every idea visually, if possible.

✦ State that evaluation of ideas is off limits for now.

✦ Ensure that every team member has the opportunity to get his/her thoughts on the table.

For now, just throw the nets out and pull in as many thoughts as possible. If the group is reluctant or seems to be having a difficult time coming up with ideas, instruct each of them to anonymously write down three possibilities on a piece of paper and hand them in; then record all of the ideas. This way, input remains confidential. This process provides a channel for the less vocal or introverted team members to have the same level of influence as more dominant members. If the facilitator's presence at the front of the group seems to be inhibiting the free flow of information and ideas, request another team member to act as a scribe.

Removing the Brakes

Be aware of obstacles that may keep the group's creative thinking from accelerating:

✦ Time pressures and impatience

✦ Evaluations and criticism from others

✦ Preformed positions/solutions

✦ Inability to shift from or focus on constraints and limitations rather than opportunities and possibilities

✦ Habitual responses or impulses

✦ Group norms and climate that repress innovative thinking

✦ Negative experience or punishment for creative thinking in the past

✦ Anxiety that comes from complex situations

✦ Reluctance to test boundaries, traditions, and conventions

✦ Inability or unwillingness to explore another viewpoint/role

Incubation

After the group exhausts its brainstorming energy, shift from an "idea generation" mode to an evaluation mode. Be careful, because the way various ideas are evaluated can either validate the open and creative process or expose it as a fraud. In other words, when eliminating ideas, it's important that the rejected ideas be discussed openly, measured against objective criteria, and then eliminated in a respectful way that supports the brainstorming that just took place. Consider this approach: "Mary, are you okay if we set aside your earlier thought since it appears that it will cost more than we've budgeted?"

Once the best ideas and possibilities have been captured, they need to be weighed and measured against the essential requirements and needs of the situation. This requires a conscious and visible shift in approach, conveying to team members that their ideas have been heard and considered, and that now they need to be judged and eliminated. If this shift isn't done in an open fashion, it can feel rather abrupt. So the  facilitator must skillfully manage and communicate this change in the work. Here's an example:

"Okay, thanks for all of the ideas — this list looks great. Now we need to shift gears and start eliminating or combining ideas. Can I ask you all to let go of ownership of the ideas you have suggested and help us objectively look at each idea, to see how it fits the needs of the situation?"

In every group, one or two awful ideas emerge, and sometimes they're suggested with serious intent by someone who may not have a grasp of the complexities of the situation. Some suggestions may appear laughable, but for a group to feel comfortable with brainstorming in the future, avoid letting concerns about a particular idea become the focal point, rather than the recommendation itself.

To address some of the less viable options, simply ask the group if some of the ideas fail to meet the essential criteria for success. If you can cluster a few of these ideas together, the ones with real potential emerge without making anyone feel exposed or threatened. "Let's step

back, and look at the list. Since we must have a solution by the end of the month, are ideas that need three months to develop options for further consideration?"

Solutions

When you begin evaluating ideas, be sure to define and display the criteria on which the decision is to be based. Don't expose the evaluation criteria during the initial brainstorming, even if they are common knowledge. When it's time to look more carefully at options and alternatives, a visible list or chart helps team members compare each alternative against the criteria. Team members are then able to see and judge for themselves, and less workable ideas become evident in the first few moments of the process.

ALTERNATIVE OR SOLUTION	CRITERIA TO BE MET			
	TIME	QUALITY	BUDGET	COMPLEXITY

A visible spreadsheet or tool enables the group to quickly identify the solutions that don't measure up to the criteria, leaving a few, perhaps two or three, that need further examination. These options may require more open discussion, research, and consideration, weighing the pros, cons, and long-range consequences of each of the final contenders.

Don't be in a rush to get to the plan; allow the best solutions to bubble up through the process. Rather than allowing the group to leap to the first obvious solution, the facilitator should continue trying to elicit comment input, and guiding the group through an evaluation of the available options. Without criticism, let the group discover, explore diverse ideas and channels of thought, and forge a quality solution that people can support.

This process can be formalized and systematic, or it can be done in a more relaxed and conversational way. Most decisions don't require a highly scientific process, although having accurate data is always helpful. The more reliable the information, the more capable and comfortable team members will feel in making the decision.

Tips for Team Members

For team members, thinking creatively means that you're willing to develop and contribute your best ideas to the work of the team. We can all spur our creative energies by looking for new alternatives, better ways to achieve our work, and being willing to synergize with others. Even if you believe you're not naturally a creative person, your knowledge, skills, and experience can help you find innovative solutions to problems.

Look at the "Big Picture"

✔ Step away from the hectic pace of the day-to-day, and try to gain a realistic perspective on how your work fits into the larger scheme of things in your organization. How do your efforts impact others on your team, in your department, division, or company?

✔ Set time aside to look for process improvements in your work. What could be done differently, better, or more effectively?

✔ Conduct an exercise to find "The Dumb Things We Do." What current practices came from old technology, old thinking, or old criteria for success?

Contribute Actively

✔ Continually talk to others in your group about their ideas. Spend time considering options and possibilities.

✔ On a regularly basis, make suggestions to your manager about ways to improve your work output, quality, or production.

✔ Engage in group discussions. Make sure your ideas, and the best ideas of others, have a chance to be heard.

CHAPTER 18

Building
Consensus

Building Consensus

When people work in groups, they commonly become polarized around two or three possible solutions. Team members have their own facts and opinions that create conflict and disagreement. Factions may emerge, and some of these sub-groups may strongly defend certain positions. This is a potentially difficult situation for the facilitator because, in the end, the group will effectively implement the solution only if every team member believes in it.

When establishing ground rules, address how to move forward in the case of an impasse. If team members understand how disagreements will be handled ahead of time, they'll be more willing to let their own "pet solutions" go. They may also be more comfortable with a prioritizing process, a straw poll, the decision to defer to the most experienced team person, or allow a rule that the facilitator to "break the tie," so to speak.

Even when the group has agreed on how a problem-solving decision should be reached, some team members may feel so strongly about a particular alternative that it is difficult to gain consensus. If time permits, allow further discussion to explore both the benefits and draw-backs of the competing solution, and the reasons for such strong resistance.

Occasionally, however, there isn't time for extended debate over the best decision. The facilitator may have to call for a vote after weighing the input from all team members. If certain team members have some

residual resentment about the decision, the challenge is to seek support and then orchestrate a consensus on how to move forward in a unified way.

How can a facilitator help all team members get behind the group's decision? Certainly, well-defined ground rules and a positive team culture help. But sometimes the facilitator may be faced with the challenge of working through heated debates and spirited discussions, gaining consensus, and exploring how the solution can best be implemented.

As in most interactions, active and genuine listening helps team members feel that their objections have been heard. Probing to ensure that valid concerns have surfaced also helps. In the final analysis, the facilitator may have to rely on personal expertise and credibility. A facilitator can build up, over time, a store of both knowledge and goodwill by listening and showing respect. These assets come in handy when a tough decision has to be made.

After all is said and before the discussion ends it's also important, that the facilitator receive clear, verbal commitments from team members to ensure that they are in agreement with the decision or direction. This type of commitment doesn't include a nod or "no comment" response; a verbalized commitment is required from every team member. At this point, some team members may still feel that there are better choices, but once the final decision is made and everyone has voiced an opinion, everyone must be willing to step up and be responsible for the mission ahead.

> "Listening, not imitation, maybe the sincerest form of flattery."
>
> *Dr. Joyce Brothers*

In some situations, the facilitator may find it helpful to start building consensus by breaking the team or the task up into smaller discussion groups. This not only speeds up the process, it also increases the level of involvement and contribution of the team members. If some team members are resistant to a decision reached by the rest of the group, perhaps they can work on another part of the task, or maybe they need some individual coaching with a member of the group or the facilitator to isolate and better define their concerns or issues. Don't be too hasty — learn to be comfortable with dissent and conflict. Differences drive creativity just as well as they polarize. Constructive tension is healthy as long as it doesn't become a personal attack. Be prepared to confront team members who hold the group's progress hostage simply because their preferences are not being selected. A facilitator's job is to ensure thorough debate, not to ensure that certain individuals get their way.

Some groups are large enough that they can take on multiple tasks at the same time by creating sub-groups for each project. By tasking team members according to abilities, opportunities for growth, and enthusiasm, the facilitator draws the best from the team's collective resources.

Even on a single project, break-out groups can be used to address components of the whole. A task force may do research, make recommendations, or accomplish specific tasks, re-convening as necessary to check progress, plan, and re-focus.

Frequent use of break-out groups provides team members with the opportunity to work with a variety of people, gain experience in different tasks and responsibilities, learn leadership and facilitation skills, and "cross-pollinate" the group with different ideas and viewpoints. Sub-groups that require a few individuals to work well together, particularly when those combinations change, build strength and diversity in the group as well.

Build Consensus Checklist

✔ Avoid defending and arguing personal preferences. Present positions as clearly and logically as possible. Listen to the reactions of the team members, and consider them carefully before you "press" a certain point.

✔ Do not assume that someone must win and someone must lose if a stalemate is reached. Instead, look for new combinations or the best alternative for all parties. Define fundamental interests and needs rather than lock onto positions/alternatives.

✔ Do not give in simply to avoid conflict in exchange for harmony. When agreement seems to come too quickly and easily, be attentive and ask questions. Yield only to another position when there is an objective, logical, or sound foundation.

✔ Avoid conflict-reducing techniques such as majority vote, averages, coin-flips, and bargaining. When a dissenting member finally agrees, don't fabricate rewards or provide future concessions.

> "To be able to ask a question clearly is two-thirds of the way to getting it answered."
>
> *John Ruskin*

✔ Differences of opinion are natural and expected. Seek them out, and try to involve everyone in the process. Disagreements help the group create a wide range of information and opinions that lead to more adequate solutions.

✔ Do not accept silence as tacit agreement. Ask team members specifically and individually if they agree or disagree. If a team member hasn't contributed, ask for that person's perspective and listen. Notice the non-verbals, engage eye contact, and draw all team members into the dialogue.

Tips for Team Members

Gaining consensus refers to the process of getting everyone "on board" with a decision. It's usually not as simple as taking a vote, and it isn't necessarily achieved when someone makes a decision and imposes it on the group. Consensus means a "meeting of the minds," where each member sees the value of the decision and finds a way to commit to its implementation. Even if it's not the preferred option for every team member, consensus is reached when the group agrees to put its best efforts into making it happen.

Presenting Your Point

✔ Be vocal with your ideas. Contribute to the brainstorming and idea-gathering process.

✔ Listen to others with respect, but don't be afraid to present opposing views and ideas.

✔ Look for synergy. Can you combine parts of one idea with parts of another to create a new and better approach?

Coming to Agreement

✔ De-personalize your evaluation of alternatives. Set your preferred option aside for a moment, and consider each choice on its merits.

✔ Vote your conscience, and defend a position you believe in, but be open and non-defensive in listing to others.

✔ Evaluate your commitment. Can you buy in to and fully support the decision that's been made?

CHAPTER 19

Go for
Action

CHAPTER 19

Go for Action

Effective groups synthesize interactions into a concrete plan of action. Although some plans are so sophisticated that they require diagrams and flow charts, the interactions discussed in this chapter simply require clearly defining desired results and how determining best to achieve these results.

Groups often refer to these results as take-away's, deliverables, products, or objectives. Some projects do require an extensive, detailed list of these items, whereas some tasks require only a verbalization of a specific commitment. Some people are left-brain thinkers and need the desired results and action steps to be clearly defined and organized into a neat, orderly list. Other people are right-brain oriented. They prefer ambiguity and flexibility in the means to reach the agreed-upon ends. The ideal situation is to find balance between the two to ensure clarity and accountability.

Action is the heart of successful business groups. Action plans convert discussion and decisions into hard-core results. The plan lays the groundwork for delegation and provides a compass for individual team members. There are three key components to effectively taking action. It is helpful to see this process as a funnel, through which discussions and decisions pass, and gradually bring focus and specificity to an action plan.

1. Consider the Action Plan in a Broad, Creative Way

Brainstorm some possible courses of action with the group. Use open-ended questions to draw out the experience and ideas of others:

+ "What do we want to have happen?"

+ "What is the target?"

+ "What needs to be done to reach the target?"

+ "How do we make this solution work?"

+ "When does this need to be completed?"

+ "What additional resources are needed in order to succeed?"

Let the ideas flow naturally, and encourage team members to think "outside the box."

+ "If there are no objectives, one can never fail."

+ "If there is no destination, one can never be lost."

2. Organize Ideas

Discuss how to bring some structure to the ideas that have been gathered. Identify similar suggestions and ideas, and cluster them into something more concrete, specific, and guiding. Ask the following questions:

+ "What is the best sequence for these action items?"

+ "Are there any steps that need to be combined or broken up into smaller steps?"

+ "Who needs to be involved?"

+ "What is the best way to follow up?"

+ "How will we measure our progress?"

+ "What is the timing for each of these items?"

This comprehensive look at action items will support future follow-up efforts and progress checks.

3. Check Your Work

Once the details of a plan are outlined, encourage team members to take a figurative step back. Look at the plan as a whole:

+ Is it realistic?

+ Can the timetables be met in light of other commitments and schedules?

+ Are there potential challenges or obstacles?

+ How will the group adapt and changing conditions?

+ Have any action items been missed?

Most projects require more than a "to-do" list: the plan must have structure, clarity, and coherence.

> "A job worth doing, be it great or small, is worth doing well or not at all."
>
> *Reed Budge*

Test the plan against the SMART criteria. Is the plan **S**pecific, **M**easurable, **A**ttainable, **R**ealistic, and **T**ime-bound? Add detail where appropriate. Communicate enthusiasm and commitment to these action items. Spark some excitement in the group to inspire team members to move forward with the action plan. Clarify, answer questions, and launch the plan with full support. Proper planning sets a course for the team's success.

Although many people do not enjoy establishing an action plan or feel inadequate doing so, action planning is also avoided for several other reasons:

1. Time — It takes an added time investment to plan. Ironically, the reason time is scarce now is because adequate time was not originally devoted to the plan.

2. Discipline — Consciously or unconsciously, people tend to keep busy with work that is enjoyable or comes easily in order to avoid less familiar or uncomfortable tasks.

3. Tracking — The plan must be recorded to provide a tracking baseline. However, writing down a plan takes effort (even though it usually improves the quality of the action plan).

4. Autonomy — Plans sometimes force a structure that people have to adhere to, and this can interfere with personal needs such as flexibility and freedom.

5. Commitment — An action plan usually ends with a commitment on the part of individuals to a specific result by a specific time. This entails accountability, exposure, and vulnerability.

Because these factors exist, the facilitator plays a critical role in helping the team come to terms with them. It can be hard work helping the group through obstacles. A facilitator needs to be alert, observant, and ready to help lead the group through a candid and open discussion when the group avoids the harsh realities of good planning.

Action Plan Checklist

✔ Identify and define "tentative" objectives early in the process.

✔ Permit subjective objectives in the initial brainstorming phase.

✔ Gather and record information, data, judgment, and assumptions to feed into the action planning process.

✔ Involve anyone who has information or expertise to offer, who will be impacted by the action plan, and who has to carry out the action plan.

✔ Divide the plan into tasks and time segments.

✔ Assign each task or responsibility to a specific individual with a specific time schedule.

✔ Review progress periodically to ensure that work is progressing and to omit those who may be struggling.

Tips for Team Members

Some of the best-laid plans fall apart at the end of the planning session. If nothing changes, or goals aren't met, planning isn't worth much. This section is about taking personal responsibility to ensure something positive is achieved.

Following Through on Commitments

✔ Review what you have agreed to do. Are you clear on what, when, where, and why?

✔ Record your commitments; create an accountable timeline for their completion.

✔ Report back at agreed-upon times. Communication is the key.

What to Do When Things Go Wrong

✔ Don't wait until it's too late. Talk to someone as soon as possible.

✔ Take responsibility both for the things that you may have missed and for helping to resolve them. Own up.

CHAPTER 20

Delegate

Delegate

Delegation is the key to putting the plan into action. Delegation allows the group to maximize resources and expertise, to accomplish more, become more efficient, and develop synergy and creativity as team members share new ideas and participate in team projects together. Delegation is a risk-taking, "stretching exercise," both for the leader who must develop the trust to "let go," and for the team members who respond to new challenges and accept additional responsibility.

> "Self confidence is important. Confidence in others is essential."
>
> *William Schreyer*

When to Delegate?

When facilitating the work of a team, the facilitator must undertake delegation as a natural part of the process. Before launching into delegation, a facilitator needs to reflect on the type of task or decision at hand. Although team involvement as is the preferred course of action as a rule, some decisions are better made by the facilitator.

The question, then, is how to decide whether or not to delegate. What criteria determine whether to facilitate and delegate or whether to maintain a greater degree of control in the decision-making process? Are there some circumstances under which it would be better to simply direct or guide the efforts of team members?

Researchers such as Vroom, Tannenbaum, and others have identified criteria that a facilitator can use to determine when and how much involvement is needed for any given decision. The following are a series of criteria that can provide some valuable guidance.

The First Screen

The first screen or set of criteria — Alignment, Correctness, and Time — provides an initial direction for the decision concerning delegation.

Alignment means that both the facilitator and team members have the same goals, objectives, and end in mind, and that either party would reach approximately the same conclusions independent of one another. When alignment exists, involve the group, because everyone wants the same basic results. If alignment doesn't exist, the facilitator may need to take a more directive approach.

Correctness means that there is one right or prescriptive answer to the question, problem, or issue. This usually means that laws, regulations, or policies dictate how the problem should be addressed. Even if the facilitator chooses to discuss the issue with the group, choices are severely restricted by the obvious "right answer" that should be chosen. When this is true, involve less and direct more.

Time refers to the urgency of the situation. Lack of time usually indicates a more directive stance, because there simply isn't time for a lot of discussion and debate on the issue.

For each of these three criteria, there is a simple question facilitators can ask to determine the level of delegation:

+ **Alignment:** Do you and your team see this issue differently?

+ **Correctness:** Is there one right or prescriptive answer to this problem?

+ **Time:** Is there urgency to this situation?

Situations that meet these criteria are usually command decisions and a more directive, less involving or delegating approach is more productive and efficient.

However, if all or most of the answers to these questions are "no," then move to the second screen of criteria.

The Second Screen

The second screen includes some additional criteria against which to measure situations or decisions and to use in determining how much group discussion, involvement, or delegation is appropriate. There are five criteria to consider: Information, Commitment, Development, Complexity, and Significance.

Information refers to how much is currently available and how much is needed. Does the facilitator know enough about this situation to feel comfortable and confident making the decision? Are other team members or groups better qualified, more educated, or more experienced than the facilitator in this area?

Commitment refers to whether or not the solution requires true "buy-in" by the group. Does it matter whether team members believe in and support the solution? Will the facilitator be able to mandate the way the situation is remedied? Will the facilitator need voluntary or discretionary motivation to sustain the remedy?

> "The quality of a person's life is in direct proportion to their commitment to excellence, regardless of their chosen field of endeavor."
>
> *Vincent Lombardi*

The third criterion, **Development**, focuses on whether the situation represents an opportunity for team members to grow, gain experience, or develop additional capacity. All else being equal, could the facilitator use this situation to help team members move to a new level of development? When development opportunities exist, use a more involving style.

Fourth, consider the **Complexity** of the situation. If the decision is cut-and-dry, or if there is a clear blueprint or template for how to succeed, a directive role may be more appropriate. However, as decisions become more complex and unstructured, it's usually wise to involve team members, to ensure you're seeing your choices clearly.

Finally, consider the **Significance** of the decision. Will this decision have long-term implications? If the decision is what color to paint the employee lunchroom, the answer may not matter much. But if the decision is more consequential, such as determining the type of computer system to install or deciding whether or not to expand the business into a new territory, the decision will have far-reaching impact, and involving, others is best.

Here are some simple questions to ask to determine whether the second screen indicates a more involving, or more directive style.

+ **Information:** Is additional information needed to make this decision?

+ **Commitment:** Will this solution require the group's commitment in order to be successful?

+ **Development:** Does this situation represent an opportunity for team members to grow and expand their capacity?

+ **Complexity:** Is this a complex decision?

+ **Significance:** Will the decision have long-term impact on or important consequences for the organization?

If the answers to these five questions are "yes" or mostly "yes," take a delegating, involving approach. If the answers are mostly "no," delegate less.

These criteria are helpful in providing a sense of direction for decisions. However, with so many criteria to consider, it may not always be clear which style to choose or how far along the "involvement continuum" to move. Delegation and involvement aren't totally scientific; they are very situational. Combine the criteria with your experience in working with the people, workload, and tolerance for risk-taking. Keep in mind that many people err on the side of too little delegation, rather than too much.

Delegation is not complicated, at least in theory. It represents an opportunity for team members to grow by assuming responsibility, while relieving the sometimes heavy task load of a leader or facilitator. The following steps provide valuable guidance when working through the "Act" phase of the facilitation process:

1. Focus on delegating one action item at a time. Ask for volunteers (if all team members are basically capable) then invite the group to recommend a team member, and finally have the facilitator select the person to carry out the task:

 ✦ "Is anyone willing to attend the council meeting?"

 ✦ "Does anyone have a suggestion as to who would be the best person to interview speakers?"

 ✦ "Pat, will you set up the conference arrangements?"

2. Clarify the assignment in broad terms to the team member(s) responsible. Establish parameters under which the task must be accomplished:

 ✦ "Lisa, we need you to seek out a supplier to provide parts for the new system."

 ✦ "The project needs to be completed by June 15th, within a budget of $15,000."

3. Connect the task to other projects or plans. Provide the linkage to other tasks that are part of a larger project.

 ✦ "Jane, when you have identified a technician, please let Mark know so he can provide the specs to the technician."

 ✦ "We're scheduled to launch Phase II in early July, and we won't be able to proceed without your task being complete. Will that work for you?"

4. Determine a time frame, needed resources, and support for the assignment. Focus on the end results rather than ways to accomplish the task.

+ "It appears that we will need the permit documents by February 15th."

+ "You will probably need to track down the records from the legal department."

5. Check for understanding and seek commitment.

+ "Do you feel you understand the assignment?"

+ "Do you feel comfortable carrying out the assignment?"

+ "Does the group have your commitment to follow through with this action item?"

6. Express confidence in and support for the team member. Help him/her feel the group's commitment to his/her success.

+ "Thank you for accepting this assignment, Joe. I am confident that you will do a good job."

7. Establish a time for follow-up, and then...follow up!

+ "Can we get together next week to see how things are going?"

+ "Will you be able to get back to me with your plan by next Friday?"

There are a few other principles to keep in mind to delegate in a way that achieves business results while helping team members grow.

Be Sure the Team Member is Up to the Task

Match people — their skills, experience, and willingness — to the assignments. Give them a fair opportunity to succeed. Listen to how they respond, or avoid responding, to their assignment. Sometimes a pat on the back and a push in the right direction are all that is necessary. Other times, team members struggle with legitimate concerns about their ability to complete the assignment, and they just don't know how to communicate that to you without it reflecting negatively on them.

Divide and Conquer

Most projects (and some tasks) require the work of more than one person. Be sure that one team member doesn't have to shoulder more of the burden than they're able to handle. Spread and share the responsibility and the risk. Pair team members according to strengths and weaknesses, sometimes allowing a less experienced individual to take the lead while being supported by a more experienced partner. Avoid breaking up the delegated components into too many pieces.

On some teams, one or two people volunteer for all the assignments. In our organization, we have a situation where one of our high-performing team members always volunteers (or gets volunteered) for action items and projects. This seems to occur naturally because she is exceptional at what she does, and everyone on the team knows that she will come through on whatever she's assigned. The problem is, she is often overworked and pulled in too many directions. This is not a healthy situation for her or for the team, but not everyone realizes this.

Ensure Consensus and Commitment

Delegation is not truly effective if people feel that they have been dumped on or pressured into accepting on an assignment. Rather than feeling like an opportunity, the task may seem like a burden. Be sure that team members can clearly verbalize what they're being expected to do. Watch for clues in their attitude; look for an enthusiastic response, tempered by a realization of the scope and challenge of the task.

Record Plans and Commitments

Create a record of what team members (and strategic partners) plan and agree to do. Identify shared responsibilities, timetables, and  desired results. A simple chart can help keep track of the progress of a single task or a collection of them that constitute a project.

Following these steps in delegating tasks and projects to team members will increase their ability to

rise to the occasion, learn new skills, and assume leadership roles. Proper planning and record keeping, along with generous amounts of support and encouragement, motivate team members to achieve new levels of productivity and responsibility.

Tips for Team Members

Team members may not have the opportunity to delegate tasks to others on a regular basis; instead tasks and assignments are delegated to them. Effective delegation requires both someone to give and someone to receive the responsibility.

Be Sure You're Clear

✔ Have you clarified your assignments? Make sure you're clear about expectations, timelines, etc.

✔ Do you feel comfortable with and capable of the assignment?

✔ Do you need additional resources or information to successfully complete it?

Negotiating Your Assignments

✔ Don't be afraid to discuss, negotiate, or restructure assignments.

✔ Communicate clearly, and be honest with yourself and others about what you can be responsible for.

✔ Ask for opportunities to stretch yourself and grow.

Facilitating the Group from Hell

CHAPTER 21

Facilitating the Group from Hell

Facilitators occasionally encounter the dreaded "group from hell." These groups are caustic and extremely dysfunctional. They may be at a point in projects and/or development where people have become angry, hostile, frustrated, or resentful. Some groups are routinely difficult, while other groups pass through periods of turmoil that can threaten to destroy them. Group disintegration can occur in families, businesses, school boards, or homeowners associations. Any time people come together, individual fears, concerns, motives, habits, and emotions emerge.

With some groups, plenty of tension is apparent right from the beginning. Visual clues, side conversations, and body language indicate obvious unease. With other groups, the tension suddenly explodes, ignited by an unexpected incendiary comment. Successful facilitators have to be constantly vigilant, ready to respond with the skill and courage required to wade into the swamp and wrestle with the alligators.

This is one of the reasons why facilitating groups is so exhausting and demanding. A facilitator has to be constantly alert to the early warning signals of trouble, and then be ready to contribute wisdom, experience, tact, and judgment to make it all work.

Before exploring the rules of engagement with difficult groups or groups at a difficult point, it is important to identify what makes a group explosive. There are main reasons and root causes for groups to be flirting on the edge of disaster.

Void of Purpose

Some groups flounder and become hostile because they lack clear priorities or direction. Consider the following analogy: Have you ever been lost, really lost, in the city, woods, etc.? Do you remember the feeling? Did you panic, become frantic or frightened? A similar process occurs with a group that has lost its bearings. Team members get frustrated, angry, and resentful. People are prone to lash out, give up, and attack ideas, plans, and other team members. Team members feel meetings and discussions are pointless, commitment and motivation suffers, and people gradually become disillusioned. Team members eventually reach a breaking point because they resent wasting their time and want to be connected to a common purpose and greater cause.

Negativity

Another phenomenon within difficult groups is negative feedback. These groups only hear about the things that go wrong, the things they aren't doing, and the ways in which they consistently come up short of expectations. People in these groups don't hear much good news or hear about progress. They don't get much credit or reinforcement for what is going well. It could be senior management, customer groups, community groups, or other departments that are dominant and aggressive. Consequently, these difficult groups feel beaten up, and unappreciated; they have a tendency to become defensive and possessive. The negativity begins to feed on itself, creating a downward spiral. Team members may start taking their frustration out on each other. People who are busy "covering it up," playing it safe, and defending themselves can make it very

> "It's like most anything. If you want to be a loser, there's always a way to dwell on the negative. If you want to win, there's always a way to think positively."
>
> *Tony La Russa*

hard on the facilitator to help move the group into a positive and hopeful frame of mind.

Assertive Personalities

Some groups are unusually difficult by the sheer nature of the people in the group. It all boils down to the personalities and the chemistry that develop between team members. Some groups may be made up of a large number of outspoken, competitive, type "A" personalities. These individuals generally try to monopolize conversations and over-control the decisions of the group. These people tend to do a lot of talking and seldom listen and digest what others have to offer. Impatient, fast-moving individuals sometimes look at "combined efforts" as a burden.

> ... In today's complex world, collaboration is not a luxury but a necessity when formulating good strategy and effective policy.

Team members joke about collaboration, complain about meetings, step in and out of discussions, and interrupt deliberations with cell phones and computers. They claim that their busy schedules don't allow them the luxury of collaboration. They can see the benefits, but they don't understand that in today's complex world, collaboration is not a luxury but a necessity when formulating good strategy and effective policy. Some people feel above the process, thinking that they are too smart to be bothered by or associate with those of lesser intelligence. It can be a challenge for the facilitator to slow down a runaway train and allow the natural synergy of the group to develop.

Timid Personalities

Groups can also be incredibly timid, shy, or withdrawn. Some team members simply don't contribute, perhaps because they have never been consulted in the past. These team members have become accustomed to keeping their mouths shut, minding their own business, and checking their brain out as they enter the workplace each day. Sometimes this habit emerges because people are fundamentally introverts. Other times, team members are uncertain or insecure about their abilities to contribute. There is nothing wrong with people who like seclusion, or privacy, or who shutter at the thought of openly stating an opinion. Sometimes, these people have not found their voice and are not comfortable with working, thinking, and sharing in an intense group situation.

These types of groups are made up of good people, with good intentions, but this doesn't make it any easier for a facilitator who has to engineer a way to involve team members. In fact, these groups often become emotional or embroiled in conflict. It is possible that they have not experienced a productive group in which people interactively blend ideas. If a facilitator can get these team members to take a risk, open up, and experience success in a group setting, wonderful ideas can emerge, unleashing a new level of commitment.

Selfishness

Similarly, some groups have team members with a strong agenda or particular ax to grind. These team members use group discussions as a forum or stage to promote an agenda, launch an attack, or covertly manipulate the agenda to their personal advantage. Some people may be in a group setting to "pay back" a prior injustice. These individuals are willing to sever group ties in order to "even the score."

Holding Grudges

In other cases, groups carry a lot of baggage from the past that they just won't let go of. Some team members are so fixated on the past that they just can't function and focus on present needs. It's like an urban legend that has developed and taken on a life of its own; rumor has it that someone did something to someone 10 years ago. Unfortunately, in far too many cases, the "it" really happened, but it has been inflated, distorted, and embellished to an unbelievable degree. Oftentimes, the "it" didn't occur to anyone in the current group. This passionate "mystery cause" becomes a major obstacle for a facilitator who must artfully disengage the group from the grip of this perceived injustice.

Conflict of Interest

Finally, some groups are stuck in a basic conflict of interests. The conflict may center on strong opposing views regarding goals, methods, values, principles, data, or interpretations of the data. The "group approach" is not always the best way to develop a solution. The time, energy, and emotional costs may not be worth taking the group through the minefields and potholes toward a decision. Unfortunately, there are times when a group isn't capable of coming together and delivering a superior win/win result. If the group is deeply divided or has competing goals, no facilitator can or should maneuver the group toward collaboration. There are times when a well-informed authority figure needs to make a firm decision.

> The "group approach" is not always the best way to develop a solution.

Lack of Time

In today's competitive, fast-paced environment, many individuals are stressed out or on the verge of burnout. This means that some people don't have the energy, concentration, or desire to give more. These people are looking for balance in their lives and see one more meeting as unfair and burdensome. People who feel the group has encroached on their lives can become resentful and angry. They are not willing to commit to the work of the group and may even fight against the purpose of the group. Occasionally, a facilitator incorrectly judges the fatigue level of a group. Heavy-duty, problem-solving tasks require adequate breaks. After about an hour of concentrated thought and discussion, the group needs a break. Without a break, people slowly give up and begin to give in when they should be committed to the process through intense discussion and debate.

Building consensus and orchestrating compromise with a difficult group are challenging to say the least. So what does a facilitator do with a group when emotions are high? How does a facilitator handle a situation when open warfare and hostility lead to an attack? How does a facilitator prevent a group from imploding on itself? Unfortunately, there is no magic formula or silver bullet. But some tools are helpful in maintaining a little grace under fire:

As a facilitator:

1. Do not take the group's outrageous behavior personally. When a group is angry, frustrated, or acting like a victim, the facilitator is an easy target or scapegoat. Discussing the facilitator or the facilitation style doesn't address the problem, task, or situation. So don't "act" slaughtered or allow the group to sacrifice you. Sometimes, facilitators need to politely walk away from "mission impossible." Not all groups can be helped. Group members have to ultimately help themselves.

> "Our greatest weakness lies in giving up. The most certain way to succeed is always to try just one more time."
>
> *Thomas Edison*

2. Adopt realistic expectations. Too many facilitators try to do magic acts and gain recognition by heroically rescuing a group that is in trouble. When a group is on the verge of crisis, there may not be a "quick fix." Many times, the best conclusion is a neutral outcome. Significant progress may not be achievable.

3. Vigorously enforce ground rules. If ground rules don't exist, establish them immediately. It is a little like driving without a license; you can get by until you get pulled over. The ground rules serve as the facilitator's license to "ticket" the group and call team members to order. A facilitator should make it clear that team members have to play by the rules. If team members don't like the ground rules, they need to be changed through group consensus. However, a facilitator should be firm and listen carefully as topics are discussed.

4. Let the group vent occasionally, while helping the group discover that crying about a situation won't help solve the prob-

lem. Sometimes, the group needs to "dump out" all of its frustrations. It is like a brainstorming session in reverse. Similar to a brainstorming session, a facilitator should write concerns on a flip chart or other visual. This reduces repetitiveness or getting on the band wagon about one topic. A facilitator can help team members stay on track by saying, "Your point is valid, and we have it written down twice already. Do you have something new to add to the list?" A facilitator should be respectful, allow freedom of expression, establish boundaries, stay neutral, and remind the group that "solution time" is just around the corner. Summarizing and paraphrasing also help create closure.

5. Don't try to eat the whole elephant at once. The problems that difficult groups face are deep-rooted. It takes time to restore equilibrium. Break the tasks and issues into parts, combine common themes, and prioritize concerns. A facilitator should point out to the group that an "offensive front" cannot be established on 12 issues. Addressing two or three issues at once is realistic and allows for a positive outcome in at least a few areas.

6. Put the group to work. Separate team members into small groups with a task such as defining the root cause, identifying preferred solutions, or prioritizing, ranking, and combining small items into common themes. At this point, the group has already vented, so there should be no more whining, looking back, or playing the victim. A facilitator should abruptly end finger pointing and lamenting, and proactively direct the group toward future goals, solutions, or attitudes.

7. Challenge the group to think about its role in and contribution to its own problems. For example, groups often complain about interference from headquarters. They don't like being micro-managed and complain that the corporate office is too "operational, rather than strategic." However, these same

groups also micro-manage people in their own facility, don't trust others, and refuse to confront their corporate leaders through constructive dialogue. Typically, groups that are really struggling own plenty of responsibility for the situation that they are in. A facilitator should help the group focus on actions within their control, such as their own choices, emotions, and behaviors. The group has to be responsible for its behavior and move forward.

8. Don't get discouraged! Be persistent, and create separation mentally. Too often, facilitators become consumed or cornered by a group. The group doesn't determine a facilitator's credibility, self-esteem, self-respect, and confidence. Facilitators should be realistic, remain positive, and have other outlets.

9. Discipline and reprimand simply and quickly. There will be times when difficult groups get facilitators riled up, disappointed, and angry. It is important not to attack or explode while leading the group into a problem-solving mode. Consider implementing the three-strike rule: If it happens once, let it slide; if it happens again, decide when and how to handle it casually and conveniently; if it happens a third time, intervene, call out the behavior, and debrief the situation immediately. Avoid using humor, and don't hint at the problem.

Tips for Team Members

Being a member of a "group from hell" can be every bit as frustrating and difficult as facilitating one. Even our best intentions and motivation can be stymied when we belong to a group with low trust, poor attitudes, unclear communication, and rampant negativity. The first challenge, of course, is ensuring that we are contributing to the solutions, not the problems. But what else can we do?

Am I part of the problem

✔ Evaluate your patterns of communication. Do you find yourself getting sucked into the "water-cooler gossip," second-guessing, or bad-mouthing the leader or others on the team? Do you ever initiate this kind of communication?

✔ Do you openly confront issues, rather than engaging in manipulative back-room discussion?

✔ Do you contribute to the effective operation of your team by giving your best effort?

Help out

✔ Most facilitators in situations like this feel isolated, burdened, and alone. Offer to take on a project or task that you know would "clear the load" for your group's leader.

✔ Don't be afraid to challenge negative behaviors or communications in the group setting. Identify or call out inappropriate language, personal attacks, or negativity.

✔ Don't get drawn into personal conflict. Focus on the behaviors you feel are unproductive or inappropriate.

Set an example

✔ Do your work well and completely without complaint.

✔ Communicate honestly and openly.

✔ Sometimes a silent example works as well as a vocal one — let your contributions, language, and quality speak for itself.

CHAPTER 22

A Few
Final Thoughts

CHAPTER 22

A Few
Final Thoughts

S ome time ago, in preparation for a senior-level management train
ing course, we interviewed several of the participants prior to the
workshop in an attempt to better understand the challenges of their
work. They talked about the significant daily issues they face, including acquisitions, mergers, important and complex product launches,
cultural and individual change, and the constant and pressing order of
the day.

These managers were clearly stressed and strained by the inces-
sant demands on their time, the imbalance they felt between work
and personal life, and the workload that filled their
plates to overflowing. However, in spite of all these
challenges and frustrations, every one of these
tough, seasoned, veteran managers seemed to be
united in one feeling: the satisfaction they received
when working with and helping their team members succeed.

Facilitating the work of groups and teams can
be alternately exhilarating and exhausting. Working with people, and helping them grow and de-
velop, is the toughest, most rewarding, and most frustrating of all of a
leader's endeavors. Facilitating the work of groups isn't something
that a leader can manipulate his/her way through, especially if a leader
is interested in helping team members grow and become something
stronger and more capable than they are today. Coercion, manipula-

> "No person can
> be a great leader
> unless he takes
> genuine joy in the
> successes of those
> under him."
>
> *W.A. Nance*

tion, and threats may get immediate results, but it won't create capacity for tomorrow.

So the challenge for leaders and managers is to accept the higher role of facilitator. Leaders need to strike an appropriate balance between delivering expected business results, and the productive, committed, and increasingly able human assets that must be developed. To facilitate is to pave the way, smooth out the bumps, and improve the chances team members have for success. A facilitator's role also includes providing opportunities for growth and development that will stretch the abilities of team members, challenge them to learn, and help them develop new skills and confidence.

We hope this book has provided some food for thought, as you consider the unique challenges and opportunities your role as leader, manager, and/or facilitator provides. We hope you've identified strengths you can leverage, and perhaps a few areas in which you see a need for improvement and change in your approach. As you proceed in your work with teams, we encourage you to find ways to draw out the best contributions they have to offer, both individually and collectively. We hope you'll find opportunities for real synergy, and come to realize that "one plus one equals three."

Most of all, our best hope for leaders and facilitators of teams is that you'll discover in real and specific ways a grand truth: Together we are better than the sum of everyone individually. Viewing teams as untapped wells of human potential, provides opportunities for personal and professional growth. Successful leaders should be measured not just by their ability to deliver results in the fires of competition and business demand, but by the way their team members are polished, tempered, and prepared to lead and contribute in the future.

Appendix

NEXT STEPS

1. Briefly review chapter headings and sections. Note the areas you may want to return to for review and more detail.

2. Complete the Facilitation Skills Self-Assessment on the following pages to understand your skill level and your beliefs about facilitation.

3. Seek feedback from teams and groups you are involved in about things you and the group do well and areas for improvement.

4. Reflect on the Sustainability Plan on the following pages to apply the information you collected.

5. Try to use the skills and concepts soon with a situation where you have a reasonable chance of seeing success.

6. Regularly revisit key chapters and the Sustainability Plan as you enhance your facilitation skills.

FACILITATION SKILLS SELF-ASSESSMENT

Circle the number that represents your response to each question.

Question	Strongly Disagree	Disagree	Neither Agree Nor Disagree	Agree	Strongly Agree
1. I am good at establishing ground rules and guidelines to help govern group behavior.	1	2	3	4	5
2. I am effective at helping groups sort through tasks and develop a clear picture of the team's purpose.	1	2	3	4	5
3. I am often at a loss when trying to orchestrate a consensus or common agreement about decisions or issues the group is facing.	1	2	3	4	5
4. I have the ability to help a group put together a set of concrete plans (action items, assignments, time frames, etc.) to ensure the group is ready to move forward.	1	2	3	4	5
5. I am effective at holding the group accountable for achieving results.	1	2	3	4	5
6. I believe it is important to create a safe environment where group members are relaxed, open, and honest and are actively contributing ideas and comments.	1	2	3	4	5
7. I hold the view that if a group lacks clarity or doesn't understand it's primary task, the team will struggle with finding success.	1	2	3	4	5
8. Given the typical level of conflict and resistance, I don't believe there is much value in trying to obtain a consensus or common commitment in group situations.	1	2	3	4	5
9. It is my opinion that at an appropriate point, a facilitator needs to assist a group in tying off the discussion and coming to closure on a plan.	1	2	3	4	5
10. I believe it is important to evaluate the group's process and the facilitator's contribution after a group's work is completed.	1	2	3	4	5

FACILITATION SKILLS
SELF-ASSESSMENT SCORING

Transfer each response from the assessment to the grid.

Question	Skills/Abilities	Question	Values/Beliefs	Model Component
1		6		Engage
2		7		Clarify
3		8		Deliberate
4		9		Act
5		10		Sustain
TOTAL		**TOTAL**		

Scoring:

Skills/Abilities

20-25 . . . . Excellent facilitation skills

14-19 . . . . Good, but look for some skills to enhance

8-13 . . . . Fair, select some areas where you can begin to make improvement

0-7 . . . . Poor, create a personal development plan to learn how to be a facilitator

Values/Beliefs

20-25 . . . . Strong beliefs in the importance of good facilitation skills

14-19 . . . . Examine your perspective in some areas about the contribution good facilitation skills can make to the success of the group.

0-13 . . . . Rethink the role of facilitator in a group's success and seek input from others

SUSTAINABILITY PLAN

In *Leading Groups To Solutions* you learned about a facilitation skills model and specific skills for effectively facilitating teams. Prepare a plan and a commitment to apply and sustain the knowledge you gained with this material.

✦ Identify two or three facilitation behaviors/skills that you do well.

✦ Identify two or three facilitation behaviors/skills that you could improve on.

✦ What are two or three ideas or goals that you could implement with your groups/teams?

✦ What specific actions steps, situations, timeframes, and/or resources are needed to support the implementation of your ideas and goals?

✦ What are some other ways to sustain your facilitation skills and keep your abilities sharp?

NOTES

NOTES

NOTES

NOTES

LEADING GROUPS TO SOLUTIONS WORKSHOP FROM CMOE

Most of the work of organizations today is done by groups or teams. Most of us will have opportunities to lead, direct the efforts, or strive to achieve results by harnessing the efforts of others, providing them with vision or guidance, and providing them with what they need to succeed. Leading groups to solutions requires insight and a unique skill set—one that many managers may not have had an opportunity to develop.

Leading Groups to Solutions provides an in-depth, interactive workshop experience that helps managers and leaders learn to evaluate their teams or groups, harness their best energy and thinking, and generate results while building relationships. The workshop is built around the concepts and model from this book.

Participants in this interactive, two-day, practical experience will:

+ Learn and practice the 5 Skills of Facilitation

+ Apply these skills to personal facilitation challenges they face

+ Develop expertise with models, tools, and processes that will help them harness the best efforts of their teams

+ Create personal action and development plans to continue to develop their facilitation skills.

Workshop Components

✔ Introduction and Objectives

✔ Exercise: Baseline facilitation skills

✔ The Five Skills of Facilitation

✔ Exercise: The Real Thing- practicing the skills of facilitation

✔ Individual feedback

✔ Application and sustainability

For more information about the Leading Groups to Solutions or other CMOE workshops and services, please call (801) 569-3444 or visit us on the web at www.cmoe.com

OTHER BOOKS FROM CMOE PRESS

✦ *The Coach: Creating Partnerships for a Competitive Edge*

✦ *Win-Win Partnerships: Be on the Leading Edge with Synergistic Coaching*

✦ *Teamwork: We Have Met the Enemy and They are Us*

✦ *Leading Groups To Solutions: A Practical Guide for Leaders and Team Members*

To order call (801) 569-3444 or visit www.cmoe.com